REAL ESTATE SALES FROM *HELL*

what you DON'T want to do when buying or selling homes, repos, probates and short-sales

—by Bob Boog—
Real Estate Broker

THS International Publishing

Published in Santa Clarita, CA. by:
THS International
P.O. Box 221283
Santa Clarita, Ca. USA 91322-1283

ISBN No. 0-9666130-8-2
First Printing: 2003
Printed in the United States of America
Library of Congress Catalog Card Number: 2003090984

Real Estate Sales from Hell
What You Don't Want to Do When or Selling Homes, Repos, Probates and Short-Sales
By Bob Boog
Editor: Robin Quinn
Cover/Interior Design:
Rosamond Grupp
NoDoubtDesign@aol.com

Other books by Bob Boog:

Selling Homes 1-2-3
Techno-Selling
Urgent *(fiction; takes place in Central America during the early 1980's)*

-WHAT PEOPLE ARE SAYING ABOUT-

Real Estate Sales From Hell

"An excellent book! *Sales From Hell* is both entertaining and educational. You'll earn more commissions, close more sales, and avoid the mistakes others make every day."

—Terry L. Mayfield,
Author of *The Customer Connection*

"A great book. Should be required reading for all realtors and anyone thinking of buying or selling real estate."

—John O'Hare,
Broker/owner, Remax of Santa Clarita

"An Informative and entertaining book which offers helpful advice for those in real estate as well as the general public."

—Charles J. Brash,
Attorney

Disclaimer

This book is designed to provide information with regard to buying and selling homes, repos, probates and short sales.

It is not the purpose of this book to print all the information that is available on this subject, but to complement, amplify and supplement other texts. You are urged to read other available books on buying and selling homes and to tailor the information from the various sources to your specific needs.

The purpose of this book is to educate and entertain. Although efforts have been made to ensure that the information provided in this book is complete and as accurate as possible, there may be mistakes made in content and typography. The author and THS International make no warranties, guarantees or representations about the accuracy or completeness of the information contained herein and specifically disclaim any implied warranties of merchantability or fitness for any particular purpose and shall in no event be liable for any loss of profit or any other damages, including but not limited to special, incidental, consequential, or other damages.

The author and THS International shall have neither liability nor responsibility to any person or entity with respect to any loss or damage caused, or alleged to be caused, directly or indirectly by the information contained in this book. What may be acceptable practice in one state or region may not be acceptable in another. Buyers, sellers and real estate brokers and agents are hereby advised to follow the laws and regulations of state and local governments as well as their real estate board(s).

The publisher and author are not engaged in rendering legal, accounting or other professional services. Before you make a decision or take an action that involves what for you is a significant amount of money or a significant risk, we strongly caution that you seek advice from a qualified professional. If legal or other expert assistance is required, the services of a competent professional should be sought.

• Table of Contents •

About Sales From Hell

Most people who write business-related books never seem to make mistakes. Ever notice that? It's like they live in a world where other folks goof up, misplace documents or act stupidly, but not them.

That's not my world. The world that I know and love is a messy place. We humans, myself included, constantly make mistakes. We often act dumb and blame others for stupid things that we do. The technology that we've invented doesn't always work very well—often at critical moments too.

In addition, the world I know moves faster and is more unpredictable then it used to be, so it's easier to blunder. Nowadays, for example, a bank will rush to change the locks on a vacant property that doesn't even belong to them. Why? Because the bank doesn't want someone to damage the vacant property. In the old days, a bank wouldn't do something like that. Still some things don't change like sophisticated buyers and sellers taking advantage of the unsophisticated. Sometimes all it takes is to make one mistake and the old saying will once again ring true: "A fool and his money are soon parted."

That's why I wrote this book—to help make a difference. I'm trying to fill in a gap of information that I believe exists in today's dog-eat-dog world of real estate. I'd like to help unsophisticated buyers, sellers and even agents become more savvy about real estate practices. To do this, I'm going to share with you some real estate stories from hell. My aim isn't to scare you, or imply that you can't sell your own house, or to show you how badly real estate is practiced, but I'm hoping you'll learn from a similar situation. My guess is that you will at least come to realize a truth noted by the great philosopher Mark Twain, when he wrote: "By trying, we can easily learn to endure adversity. Another man's I mean." Or another truth mentioned by the philosopher Charles M. Shultz who wrote: "No problem is too big to run away from."

At this point, you may be wondering who am I to write such a book. For those of you who don't know me, my name is Bob Boog and I'm a licensed real estate broker and owner of a small real estate company. I've been selling real estate full-time for over twenty-five years in Los Angeles, California, and I've sold more than a thousand homes. In addition, I've written a book about selling homes called *Selling Homes 1-2-3* that was first published in 1998 and has since become a modest success. I have ridden the highs and lows of the real estate market and have survived. In other words, the stupidity is strong within me. What I've noticed is that many people enjoy learning about the blunders that other folks have made. After all, the next best thing to your own experience is learning from another person's, isn't it?

Hopefully you will gain some knowledge from these tales, whether you are new in real estate, looking to sell your own home, buying a home, or working as a loan officer. It doesn't matter if you're already an experienced real estate agent, or interested in real estate as an investment. Perhaps you live in an area where lawyers or solicitors handle the paperwork instead of escrow and title officers. No problem. Maybe you're just interested in reading these stories to gain more insight into real estate. That's fine too.

Some of the mistakes made in these stories may apply to where you live—others may not. In any case, what I have found is that it usually doesn't help to pass judgment when somebody else goofs up. After all, to err is human. So remember the old saw, when you point at another person, there is one finger pointing at him or her and four fingers pointing back at you.

Who knows? Perhaps one day a situation may arise that may remind you of one of the stories in this book, and maybe a little alarm will go off inside your head. Possibly this book may help someone avoid a similar sale-from-hell situation or help you realize that what seems to be misfortune can actually be a blessing in disguise. Perhaps this book will even help you to save some time. And as the old saying goes, time is money, isn't it?

Also, as you are reading this book, you may suddenly be reminded of a sale from hell that you would like to share with the world so that others might benefit from your experience. If so, please feel free to drop me a line at **www.salesfromhell.com.** I'd certainly enjoy hearing from you!

Warmest regards,

Bob Boog

LESSON ONE

BEWARE OF "PLAYING DUMB"

A FRIEND OF MINE was driving to Las Vegas with his ten-year-old son when he noticed a car parked along the side of the road. My friend casually glanced over and then realized that the vehicle belonged to a California highway patrolman. He quickly slowed down because there was a patrolman sitting inside the car holding a radar gun. Quicker than a mongoose can grab a snake, the highway patrolman turned on the red lights on his patrol car's roof and pulled my friend over.

The officer, a clear-eyed, athletic-looking fellow, hopped out of his car and slowly approached my buddy's vehicle. Then he gestured for my friend to roll down the window.

"Do you know how fast you were going?" the patrolman asked once the window had been rolled down.

"No sir, I have no idea," my friend answered.

"You have no idea?" repeated the patrolman suspiciously.

"No sir, I have no idea whatsoever," said my friend playing dumb.

"Yes you do, Daddy," piped up a helpful little voice from the backseat. "You just told me you were going 92 miles per hour!"

I mention this story because many real estate sales from hell originate from people playing dumb—like my friend talking to the highway patrolman. Playing dumb is a common thing to do, don't you agree? We all play dumb. Myself included. Which leads me to our first lesson in real estate. That is, in real estate, playing dumb may be easy to do and it may seem tempting, but this can sometimes lead to a story from hell.

"I NEVER SAID THAT!"

Mr. and Mrs. Meyers signed a purchase agreement to sell their house, and their contract called for a January 15th closing date. On or about January 5th, ten days before escrow was due to close, Mr. Meyers received a telephone call from his listing agent, Billy Beck.

"Mr. Meyers, I've got some good news and bad news," said Billy. "The good news is that the buyers' loan has been approved."

"Thank goodness. What's the bad news?"

"The bad news is that their loan broker says that we need to extend the closing date by two weeks in order to season the buyers' down payment money. Therefore, if it's all right with you, we would like to close escrow on or about January 29th instead of January 15th. Would that be okay with you?"

"Yes, that should be fine," Mr. Meyers agreed.

"Excellent," said Billy and he hung up the phone.

At this point, Billy the agent should have called escrow to amend the closing date to January 29th, right? But Billy got busy and forgot about doing it.

Like most men, Mr. Meyers is a bit absent-minded and he failed to notify his wife about Bill's telephone call and the change in settlement date. What about Mrs. Meyers? Like most women, she plans ahead. She called all the utility companies and scheduled the services to be turned off on

January 15th. She did this because she planned to stay with her sister for the next two weeks and figured that her husband would forget about turning off the utilities.

On the evening of January 16th, Mr. Meyers came home late from work. He was cold, tired and hungry. Since his wife was away visiting her sister, Mr. Meyers sat down on the sofa with a tray of food intending to watch a show about monster trucks on ESPN. Fifteen minutes into the program, Mr. Myers abruptly found himself without heat, electricity or TV on one of the coldest nights of the year.

The following day, Billy Beck received an angry phone call from Mr. Meyers.

"Mr. Beck, why hasn't my escrow closed?" Mr. Meyers demanded. "We were supposed to close escrow on January 15th, and so my wife had all the utilities shut off."

"Mr. Meyers, don't you remember? We talked about changing the closing date ten days ago. You'd agreed that closing escrow on January 29th was acceptable."

"I never said anything of the kind. Our contract called for closing escrow on January 15th, and if the buyer can't perform, than I want out of this deal. I've suffered damages as a result of this buyer not being able to close on time. He'll have to pay for a hotel room for me, from now until closing, plus kennel storage for my two dogs. Yada, yada, yada."

Now, regardless of whose fault it is, can you see how easy it is to play dumb? Do you see how playing dumb can lead to a hellish story?

BOB'S BOTTOMLINE In order to be enforceable, any and all changes to the original purchase agreement should be confirmed in writing by both parties. However, the reality is that nowadays closing dates often change. Why? Because stuff happens. So the truth is that many times the settlement does not close on the exact date specified in the original contract. Buyers and sellers may even sign a disclosure regarding the possibility that there is a chance of not closing on time.

In the Meyers transaction, Billy Beck pointed out some fine print to his client. The sentence read: "The complexity of a real estate transaction may necessitate an extension of the closing date which should be in writing signed by Buyer and Seller. However, it is suggested that Buyer and Seller remain as flexible as possible with regard to all plans based on an exact closing date." In this case, because Mr. Meyers had already signed this disclosure, he didn't have a leg to stand on when he played dumb. Mr. Meyers simply had to turn his utilities back on and waited for the close.

HONEYMOON HORROR

Davy Jones was a clean-shaven, forty-year-old, blue-jeaned computer programmer, and his girlfriend Cheryl Johnson was a blonde beauty in her early thirties. They wished to purchase a condominium in our area, and before taking them out in my car, I had their credit checked by a local loan broker. The loan broker said, "Cheryl Johnson has excellent credit. Find her a condo today and write it up."

We found the perfect condominium. However, before writing up the contract, I learned that although Cheryl Johnson had excellent credit, she hadn't been on her job very long. And Davy's credit was so bad it smelled like rotten soybeans. Since Cheryl's income wasn't strong enough for her to purchase the condo on her own, we needed to find a co-borrower with good credit and a steady income to take Davy's place.

"No problem," Davy said, "I'm sure my old man will co-sign for me. He's got a great income, plus solid gold credit. This sale is a sure thing."

True to his son's word, Davy's father agreed to co-sign with Cheryl.

After obtaining the credit report, the loan broker called me and actually sounded amazed. "Wow!" he exclaimed, "Davy's father has the best credit I have ever seen in fifteen years of making loans."

"So there is nothing that would hold up the closing?" I asked the loan broker.

"No sir," he answered. "This sale is solid as a rock."

"The listing agent says that the seller wants to move out of the place to leave it vacant for the buyer. That's why we want to make sure that there is nothing that can go wrong."

"Well, the only thing that could possibly foul up the

closing would be if Davy and Cheryl were to get married," the loan broker admitted.

"Why would that be a problem?"

"Well, with this loan program," he explained, "the credit of the spouse must be included in the debt ratio. And Davy has stinky credit. So as long as they don't get married prior to closing escrow, Davy's credit won't be counted."

"Do they know this?" I asked.

"Oh yes," the loan broker assured me. "I told them emphatically, whatever you do, do not get married prior to closing. Just wait for escrow to close, then get married. Because if you get married in the state of California, we're going to find out about it."

"Okay, that's good," I said.

Can you guess what Davy and Cheryl did prior to closing escrow?

One night they drank too much champagne, flew to Las Vegas, and got married.

A few days before escrow was supposed to close, I received an emergency page from my loan broker. "You're not going to believe it," he said when I called him. "Cheryl's loan got declined."

I nearly choked on my cup of Starbucks mocha. "What!? You told me this was a sure thing!"

"The lender did a last-minute credit report," he explained. "A search of public records showed that a Cheryl Johnson with the same social security number as our Cheryl Johnson was issued a marriage license in Clark County, Nevada, seven days ago to a Davy Jones."

"No way," I moaned. "They know better than that. There must be some mistake." I called Davy and asked him about the situation. What did Davy do? He played dumb.

"The loan broker said we couldn't get married in California. He never talked about Nevada."

Everything fell apart because these two lovebirds couldn't wait one more week to get married!

BOB'S BOTTOMLINE As Groucho Marx said, "Marriage is a wonderful institution, but who wants to live in an institution?" Actually, maybe it's more appropriate to say, to err is human. In this case, about two years after their condo sale didn't go through, the real estate market dropped dramatically and these two lovebirds were able to purchase a house! So even though the landscape looked torched, things eventually worked out for the best down the road. Believe it or not, these two people are still married and now have two beautiful children!

DETAILS, DETAILS

Most people know the difference between a "sellers market" and a "buyers market," but let me briefly mention the difference between the two for those of you who don't know these terms.

In a *sellers market* or "hot market," there are many people looking to buy and few houses available. Prices tend to rise and buyers tend to bid competitively. The competition between buyers often helps sellers to get higher prices: that's why it's a seller's market.

A *buyers market* or "cold market" is when there are many homes listed for sale but only a few buyers who can afford to buy. Usually the market is slower and it's a competition between sellers to reduce their prices in order to attract that hard to find buyer: that's why it's called a buyers market.

When I first started in real estate, I met some buyers named James and Helen who wished to purchase a home. The market was hotter than the frigging Sahara and there were few homes available to show, so I drove James and Helen to three different homes and encouraged them to write an offer on each place.

James was a tall, robust man who wore his thick black hair slicked back like Elvis and Helen looked like a beautiful trophy wife. James worked for the motion picture studios and made a ton of money. He said his credit was excellent and fortunately James brought an old TRW credit report, which proved that he did indeed possess excellent credit.

The house that they both liked was listed for $350,000, and with the hot market, we made a full-priced offer of $350,000.

That same day, the sellers received two other offers and a bidding war erupted. The price went from $350,000 to $360,000, and eventually James and the seller settled on a price of $362,000. Life seemed good.

Underline the word "seemed."

From the get-go, James and Helen appeared to be married, and I never asked them, "Are you married?" On the title company information sheet, James wrote that his marital status was "married," and where it asked for information about prior marriages, James had written "none."

Based on this information, I assumed that James and Helen were married.

Wrong!

Three days after the seller's acceptance, I received a telephone call from the lender. "Did you know that James is currently going through a divorce?" the loan person asked me.

"No," I said.

"Well he is, so we'll need to get a quitclaim deed from his spouse. Plus this guy shows very little money on his self-employed tax returns. He may need to get a co-signer."

First things first. In California, any buyer who is still legally married needs to have his or her spouse execute a quitclaim deed. This document gives up any interest the spouse might have from the person buying the home. A quitclaim deed was important for James because California is a community property state. This meant that any property that James purchased while legally married automatically would become half-owned by his spouse.

When confronted about the divorce, James admitted that he was indeed involved in a divorce but that he and his spouse were still on excellent terms. "She will happily sign any papers needed in order for me to buy a house," he boasted. "The two of us get along better now than when we were married."

Guess what happened?

James' friendly wife refused to sign the quitclaim deed. Then James tried to get his new girlfriend, Helen, to buy the house for him, but Helen's credit was too shaky. Luckily, as soon as we discovered that James wasn't divorced, we relayed that information to the seller who insisted that James obtain a quitclaim deed within ten days. Because James wasn't able to obtain that document from his wife, the seller was still able to sell his home to one of the other two buyers.

BOB'S BOTTOMLINE Do you see how this could have been a real sale-from-hell- story if the seller had already made plans to purchase another house and then found out at the last minute that James couldn't get his quitclaim deed? If you are a purchaser who is getting divorced and are buying a home in California and/or any other community property state, realize that you will need to get a quitclaim deed signed by your spouse before escrow can close.

MISSING IN ACTION

Kimberly Thomas arrived in California by way of Georgia. A pretty woman with bouncy auburn hair and large blue eyes, Kim spoke with a southern drawl as slow as honey. She came to an open house on a home that I had listed and immediately fell in love with the place. At that time, Kim was dating a man who lived in Pittsburgh, Pennsylvania but she had completed all the necessary loan paperwork to purchase a home in California anyway. She only needed a clean termite report and an appraisal to order loan documents.

In this case, I happened to be the listing agent as well as the selling agent, and in a counter offer, the seller requested that Kim close escrow on or about February 12th. "No problem," said Kim. "I have all of my moving boxes ready and closing escrow on February 12th will be a piece of cake."

On or about February 9th, I left Kim a message on her voice mail to remind her that she would need to bring a cashier's check to escrow in order to close by the twelfth, but she never called me back. Then she never came into escrow to sign her loan documents. I left several messages on her cell phone and at her work on Feb 9th, 10th, 11th, and 12th, but got no reply to any of those phone calls either.

The seller started getting worried as he was purchasing another home out of state, and the realtor on that transaction was frantic, wondering what was happening. The pressure was on and I had no idea how to get in touch with Kim. Finally, I sent Kim an e-mail, and I did get a response. Can you guess who just had to go to Pittsburgh for Valentine's Day?

Ah love! When Kim returned the following Sunday night, she played dumb. She said, "Oh. You mean the house isn't mine yet? I didn't know I still had to bring money into escrow and sign some more papers."

Yeah, right. Nice try.

BOB'S BOTTOMLINE If you're planning to take a trip out of town during the week of settlement, let everybody know in advance. Also, there is a document called a "Power of Attorney" which allows you to appoint another person to sign legal documents on your behalf. The Power of Attorney form can be drawn by an escrow officer, a lawyer, or a title officer, and you will need to sign it before a notary public. But by doing so, you can now leave for a trip and escrow would close while you're away. By letting people know your plans in advance, you can have your cake and eat it too!

THE DEVIL MADE ME DO IT

John and Marge Becker were selling their home "by owner" to save the real estate commission. Because the real estate market was hot, they received multiple offers. One offer was signed by Mr. and Mrs. Kim, an Asian couple, and the other offer came from Mr. and Mrs. Sanchez, a Hispanic couple. Both offers were for full price with closing in thirty days.

"Which offer should we accept?" Marge asked her husband.

"I've got an idea. Let's accept both offers," John suggested.

"Can we do that?" She wondered aloud.

"Why not?" John reasoned. "When we bought this house, the real estate agent told me that there was another family interested. I figure that if we do this right, neither family will know about the other offer. We can open one escrow at ABC escrow and the other at CBX escrow. The first one to close escrow gets the property!"

"But what if the other couple finds out?"

"If the other couple finds out, we'll just play dumb. What can they do?"

John opened both escrows as planned, but by a strange twist of fate, both escrow companies contacted the same title company to obtain title insurance. The title officer was puzzled when he reviewed the two title orders on the same property for two different buyers, so he placed a call to Mr. and Mrs. Becker.

"What the hell is going on here?" the title officer demanded to know. When John explained his plan, the title officer shook his head in disbelief on the other end of the line. "John, you can't sell your house to two different parties at the same time. It doesn't work like that."

"What should we do?" asked Mr. Becker.

"Simple. You've got to rescind one of the contracts, and cancel that escrow," the title officer advised.

Rescinding the contract and canceling escrow was easier said than done. The hot real estate market meant that there wasn't much available inventory and both buyers felt that they were entitled to the property. After all, both parties had signed legally binding contracts with the Beckers, and both families wanted to purchase the house. A standoff ensued. Tempers flared. Things got ugly.

After three months of stressful negotiations, a similar home came up for sale in the neighborhood for $20,000 more than the Beckers' home. The Beckers agreed to pay the Sanchez family a cash settlement of $20,000 which they could use to purchase the other house, contingent upon the Kims' closing escrow on the Beckers' property.

The Kims eventually did close escrow on the Beckers' property and the Sanchez family bought their new home too. The Beckers were relieved to be over with the ordeal.

BOB'S BOTTOMLINE To guarantee peace of mind when selling a home by owner, don't play dumb. Instead, talk to an expert such as a lawyer or real estate broker and have him or her review the paperwork *before* approving the contract(s).

My wife and I were selling our house by owner and so when she asked me if I could make up the sign by using a large black magic marker, I said, "Sure honey, no problem."

After putting the sign up, I did some errands around the house and my wife went to do some grocery shopping. After she came back to the house, she had a big smile on her face. "I think we're the only people selling their home who are really honest," she said. "I mean brutally honest."

"Why do you say that?" I remarked.

"Because you forgot the 'n' in owner," she told me.

Sure enough, I had written "For Sale By Ower."

—***Anonymous***

JAILBIRD SELLER

John and Juanita Ward were a middle-aged couple who were interested in purchasing a home in the best neighborhood in town. We found a lovely home that met all of their needs. When we asked Mrs. Seller where she was moving, Mrs. Seller told us that she'd been involved in a messy divorce but not to worry, that the house had been granted to her in her divorce decree. After writing a contract on the house, I was a little puzzled when we received a counter offer back from the seller that stated, "Sale is subject to Mr. Seller's approval."

"Why would the seller write that it's subject to her husband's approval?" my buyers wondered aloud. "Didn't she just tell us that she got the house in her divorce decree?"

I got a little tongue-tied but I told the buyers not to worry. After all, I reminded them that if the house had been given to Mrs. Seller by the court, she could show the escrow company the divorce decree to prove that the house was hers. With that in mind, my buyers signed the counter offer and we opened escrow.

After receiving a set of escrow instructions, I noticed that there was a place for Mr. Seller to sign so I called the listing agent. "Does our contract need to be signed by the husband?" I asked.

"No," she answered. "Mrs. Seller won the property in her divorce settlement, however the attorney suggested I write the phrase, "Subject to the husband's approval," just in case the title company requires his signature. Besides, Mr. Seller is in jail, so it won't be too difficult to find him."

"That's good," I said.

Three days before closing, escrow called me. The officer gave a six-word sentence that every real estate agent dreads hearing: "I think we have a problem."

Guess who still had to sign our contract? That's right, Mr. Seller. Even though Mrs. Seller had won the property in her divorce settlement, the title company insisted that Mr. Seller had to sign a quitclaim deed before they would issue a title policy against the property. So a notary public was sent to the prison with the quitclaim deed, but Mr. Seller played dumb.

"This isn't my house anymore, so why should I sign anything for that witch?" he said with a crooked grin. "You can't make me sign that piece of paper. You can tell my ex-wife to stick that deed where the sun don't shine!"

This really could have been a sale from you-know-where, because Mr. Seller was truly belligerent. He did not wish to make things easy for his ex-wife. However, as ill luck would have it, because Mr. Seller was also a compulsory guest of the state of California, he couldn't do very much about thwarting his ex-wife's desires. One day, at a quarter past ten in the morning, Mr. Seller jangled into court wearing wrist and ankle shackles, handcuffs, and dressed in a snappy orange prison jumpsuit. When Mr. Seller was asked by the judge to sign the deed, Mr. Seller went off on a tirade filled with enough profanity to satisfy any hip-hop songwriter. I guess he figured all that cursing would help him to further express to the judge why he shouldn't have to sign the document.

But the judge didn't see it that way. Instead, he admonished Mr. Seller for using improper language in his courtroom, then tacked a few more days to Mr. Seller's sentence for "contempt of court." Finally, the judge announced, "The court will hereby sign the contract on behalf of Mr. Seller."

The gavel sounded, Mr. Seller was led away, and our sale closed a few days later.

BOB'S BOTTOMLINE If you have become the owner of a property as a result of a divorce decree, there is a possibility that your ex-spouse may need to sign a document for a title company, so ask an attorney about this issue before your "ex" vanishes from your life. Your ex-spouse may play dumb as did the person who appeared in court wearing wrist and ankle shackles, handcuffs and an orange prison jumpsuit.

AGENT FROM HELL

Laura and Jesus Solorio arrived in town in mid-October and were looking to purchase a home for under $200,000. Their agent, Dale Carter, showed them several lukewarm properties, so Laura decided to investigate on her own to see if Dale might have missed something. She found a new home being built by a builder for $180,000, and asked Dale if he could represent them in the purchase of it.

"You don't want to buy that house," Dale advised.

"Why not?"

"Somebody at my office told me that there are already three offers on it."

"Oh well, in that case, forget it."

Later, the Solorios purchased an older fixer-upper home on the east side of town that Dale had found for them. A few months afterwards at a Superbowl party, the Solorios were talking real estate with a man named Mike who casually mentioned that he had purchased a home and his agent was Dale Carter."

"What a coincidence," Laura remarked. "We purchased our house from Dale Carter too. We found a cozy fixer-upper for only $171,000 on the east side of town."

"You ought to see my new home," Mike raved "It's a brand new home on the west side of town where the blue-ribbon school is located. Best of all, I only paid $165,000 for it."

Curious, Laura and Jesus visited Mike's new home and were horrified to discover that the house was the same one that Laura had located during her scouting mission.

"When did you buy this home?" Laura asked.

"I wrote the offer at the beginning of November," said Mike after thinking for a moment.

"How did you get such a good deal?"

"Dale told me that the builder hadn't gotten any offers on the property," Mike explained. "Dale encouraged me to write a low-ball offer to see what would happen."

Laura's blood boiled. After all, Mike is Caucasian and Laura and her husband are both Hispanic. She felt that she had been discriminated against by Dale, so the next day, she called Dale on the telephone. "You sold the house that I wanted to Mike! You knew we wanted it too, you dirty, double-dealing racist."

What did Dale do? Dale played dumb. "You never told me to write up a contract on it," Dale argued. "Heck, I don't have a racist bone in my body. If you really had wanted to buy it, I would have sold it to you in a New York minute."

Laura filed a discrimination complaint with the Fair Housing board and won! She also filed a lawsuit against Dale and won. But winning both cases meant little as Dale had no money, and it didn't appease the pain in Laura's heart for the house that she lost. Her only satisfaction was that Dale lost his real estate license and can't do the same thing to someone else.

BOB'S BOTTOMLINE Buyers and sellers aren't the only ones who play dumb. Some real estate agents play dumb too, so remember to get things in writing. For example, if you are told that a house is already "pending" or "has an offer" by your real estate agent, and you really are interested in it, ask to see written proof! If the agent can't provide a printout that shows the pending status, have the agent write up a contract and request that the agent give you an acceptance, a rejection or a written counter-offer from the seller. As Louis B. Mayer once said, "Verbal counter-offers are worth the paper they're written on."

LESSON ONE FINAL COMMENTS

All real estate contracts and addendums need to be in writing to be enforceable. A good real estate agent and a competent attorney are valuable assets in the sale of property as they can help smoke out buyers and sellers who like to "play dumb."

LESSON 2

CONFIRM THINGS LIKE COLUMBO

I ONCE ATTENDED a seminar where the sales instructor suggested that most people who buy or sell real estate could learn a lot by observing television detective Lieutenant Columbo. You remember Columbo, don't you? The short detective who worked in Los Angeles yet insisted on wearing a rumpled trenchcoat to work? Since it hardly ever rains in Los Angeles, Columbo's trenchcoat made about as much sense as a kamikaze pilot wearing a helmet. However, I think that watching Lieutenant Columbo to learn about buying or selling real estate is a good idea.

For those of you who have never watched an episode of *Columbo,* each film normally opens with a killer committing a murder, so we the audience know the identity of the killer. But Detective Columbo doesn't. Columbo is summoned to the scene where he inspects for clues. Usually the killer is smart and laughs at Columbo's mistakes and bumbling approach. But Colombo is no dummy. First he establishes rapport with the killer by calmly yacking about Mrs. Columbo and/or his life experiences. Columbo then asks a lot of questions and often writes down notes in a tiny notepad. He often prefaces questions with the phrase, "Oh, one more thing," as if the thought had just occurred to him, but usually these questions contain the very clues for solving the case. By the end of the program, naturally Lieutenant Columbo has not only figured out who committed the crime, but how it was done.

Whenever you are buying or selling a home, you want to be like a junior Detective Columbo. Not because there may have been a murder that's taken place at a property. It's just that most people love surprise endings and brilliant little twists in books, movies and on TV, but hate these surprises in real life. Especially in real estate. When something unexpected happens after people move into a property that they've just purchased, these people get angry. And if something unexpected was known by a seller who was trying to get away with something—it can often lead to a sale from hell! So the lesson to learn in this chapter is to learn to confirm things like Columbo. Do a little extra investigative work whenever you buy or sell real estate!

THE BARKING DOG

Tim and Jennifer Barr were interested in purchasing a home in the Summit neighborhood. In this exclusive area, homes sell quickly. So when I saw a house priced $20,000 below market, Tim and Jennifer quickly snapped it up. Four days after the contract was signed by the seller, the Barrs paid for a home inspection which revealed only a minor problem with the house—a leaky sink.

The next day, the transfer disclosure statement arrived. This document is a statement from the seller where he or she reveals any material facts about the house or neighborhood that might lead a purchaser away from purchasing the home if he or she had known about it beforehand. On this disclosure, the seller stated, "Noise problems from the neighbors." I suggested that Tim play Columbo and patrol the house at various times of the day and night to figure out what the seller was referring to regarding the noise.

The previous morning during the home inspection, however, the neighbor's dog had howled nonstop, almost like he was personally trying to sabotage my deal. So Tim automatically thought that the problem was the dog. "Remember the dog that never stopped barking?" he said. "That's our noise problem. That dog didn't stop barking for five minutes."

Two weeks after escrow closed, however, I got a call from Tim. "Remember how I originally thought the noise problem was caused by the barking dog?"

"Barking dog? What barking dog?" I joked.

"Let me tell you something. That dog's nothing, compared to the racket made by the weird teenage kids who live three doors away. They play in a punk rock band, and practice every Saturday afternoon at three o'clock."

"Have you complained to the city about it?"

"Nah. We've just made it a point to see a movie every Saturday afternoon."

BOB'S BOTTOMLINE

BOTTOMLINE When buying a home, don't be afraid to do some extra footwork. Confirm like Columbo. Check with the neighbors to see if there are problems that a licensed home inspector might have missed or a seller might not wish to disclose. For example, ask the neighbors if there are any underground storage tank problems, nuisance problems, insect infestations or child molestors. You may be glad you did!

THE DEAD BROTHER

Joe and Isabel Mahoney purchased a condo together. Because they were brother and sister, and neither one was married, their real estate agent suggested that they hold title as "tenants in common."

Five years later, Joe died of a massive heart attack, and six months after his death, Isabel decided to sell the property. A buyer offered her $300,000 all cash on one condition: the buyer needed a fifteen- day settlement. Isabel quickly signed the contract, however a few days later, a title officer informed Isabel that Joe Mahoney's interest in the property will have to go through probate court which might take several months to complete.

Why? Because Joe and Isabel had purchased the home as "tenants in common" and not as "joint tenants." The difference between these two ways of holding title is that joint tenancy offers the right of survivorship. In contrast, under "tenants in common," a probate court had to determine who got Joe Mahoney's share of the property. Under "joint tenancy" Joe's share would have automatically transferred to Isabel Mahoney upon Joe's death because she was the surviving joint tenant. She would still need to file a "death of joint tenant affidavit" at the County Recorder's office, but that is simple and easy to do.

BOB'S BOTTOMLINE Your community or state may offer different ways of holding title to property you purchase. The point is to play Columbo to find the best way for you to hold title. Even if escrow has already closed, you can still change the way you hold title, so check with your attorney or tax advisor for the best possible way.

Think about the consequences if one or both of you should die. Would you want the property to go through probate court? So play Columbo and get a good tax attorney's advice.

SOUR HEART

I once got a call from a man named Clyde Johnson who had a disagreeable personality. Clyde was like someone who had gotten some bad news during the Nixon administration and had never really gotten over it. The Vice President of a fortune 500 company, Clyde had upgraded and added on to his home which had reduced the size of his backyard to the size of a large concrete patio. And unexpectedly, the hot real estate market turned colder than the Ice Age.

I showed Clyde all the comparable sales. His home was currently worth $250,000 due to his lot size and the frosty market conditions. However, Clyde was such a bossy person, he almost kicked me out of his house when I told him the truth. "How dare you insult me," he thundered. "My home is worth at least $20,000 more than the Joneses' house. The Joneses' house was similar to mine and sold for $250,000 a few months ago. I know that my house is much nicer than that rat-trap! I'm hopeful to have this home sold within a week!"

So what did I do next? I folded. I told Clyde EXACTLY what he wanted to hear and listed his house for $270,000. It's true. In the real estate business, you can always find someone who will take a listing at any price. In this case, that person was me.

That's when my real nightmare began.

Two weeks later, Clyde's house had not received a single showing. Not even a lookie-loser or a nosey-neighbor to snoop around at Clyde's palatial estate. Guess whose fault that was? Mine. Clyde Johnson burned my ears telling me how quickly he had sold his other three homes.

So what did I do? I vanished. It's true. I became as invisible as a waiter at a fancy restaurant. I made sure that Clyde could never get hold of me. If he called me at home, "I was in the shower." When he called me at work, "I was out with a client" or "I'd just stepped out," or "I was in a meeting." Which probably peeved Clyde to no end.

But then, suddenly, Clyde started to get smarter about the local real estate market. He became a junior Columbo. Every day he was out patrolling the neighborhood in his car or browsing the classifieds looking at houses listed for sale. I think that, like Columbo, he wore a rumpled trenchcoat and stuck an unlighted cigar in his mouth.

Finally, one day Clyde actually got hold of me. Surprisingly, he wasn't angry at me. Why? Because I was still communicating with him via the US Postal Service. He had received two letters from me each week. Anyway, Clyde said, "Did you know that there's another house like mine for sale over on Dalbey Drive? How much do they want for that house?"

"$245,000," I answered.

"Why so low?" he whined.

"Because that's the current market value."

Within two weeks, the house for $245,000 had sold. But my nightmare wasn't over. Clyde called me and left me this message: "Bob, reduce my price."

Believe it or not, I returned that phone call in record time! "What price are you thinking?" I asked quickly.

"What price do you recommend?" he answered.

I knew it was a trap, but I didn't care. "250,000," I said.

"Are you out of your friggin' mind?" he yelled. Clyde told me to reduce the price by five thousand dollars. Now we were at $265,000 but then another new listing hit the market. The price? $242,500. Why? Because the market was going down, not up!

And after the house for $242,500 sold, Clyde reduced his price to $255,000 but guess what happened?

Clyde then called me seventeen times to complain about all the people showing his house. That's right. Before he was angry because nobody was showing it, and now he was mad because too many people wanted to see it!

"People are driving me crazy!" he yelled. "Agents are calling me at dinnertime wanting to show the house. Agents call me at eight-thirty on Sunday morning to show the house. People are begging to show the house at nine-thirty at night too. Why don't I have any offers?"

I cleared my throat. "Mr. Johnson, do you know why people want to show your house so badly?"

"Because I'm priced so low?"

"No sir, the main reason people want to show your home is so that they can sell other houses!"

"What?"

Clyde didn't want to believe it, but in a down market, agents will either ignore an overpriced listing or they'll show it day and night. Why? **Because showing an overpriced listing helps them to sell other houses!**

After five months on the market, Clyde's hopeful house finally sold for $245,000—which was probably less than what he would have received had he priced it competitively at the start.

BOB'S BOTTOMLINE To avoid the hell of overpricing a home in a slow market, even if you're selling your home "by owner," do some detective work first. Don't rely on anyone else's figures. Ideally, Clyde and I should have played Columbo before listing the house. I should have taken Clyde out in my car and had him personally see the competition and personally check out the comparative sales data. Live and learn.

MISSING CONTRACTOR

Mark and Cindy Owens always dreamed of living in their own custom home. So after purchasing a vacant lot, they called Cut-Rate Builders, a contractor that they felt would do a good job. After all, Cut-Rate Builders advertised incessantly on talk-radio programs.

Because Mark and Cindy are busy people, they didn't mind that it took about six weeks for the Cut-Rate Builder salesperson to bring them a set of plans. The couple happily cut a check for 30% of the job amount, and waited for the construction to start. After waiting for two weeks, Cindy called the contractor on the telephone. The Cut-Rate Builder salesperson told her that the work should begin shortly.

A few weeks later, the footings were inspected by the local building inspector, but then all work came grinding to a halt. A call to the Cut-Rate builder office got no response, nor did e-mails to their Web site, so Mark and Cindy decided to visit Cut-Rate Builders in person. Peeking through the darkened window, they could barely make out an empty office. The place looked deserted except for six telephones sitting on the tiled floor!

Mark called a friend who also having a custom home built. "Did you choose to have your home built with Cut-Rate Builders?" Mark asked his friend. "Oh no, I heard they closed their doors two weeks ago. They ripped somebody off for thirty-five thousand dollars and it finally caught up to them."

Mark and Cindy's dream home had turned into a not-so-funny nightmare!

BOB'S BOTTOMLINE Before hiring a contractor, get three estimates and then play Columbo. Check into the contractors' licenses to see if there are any complaints or pending litigation. Find out how long the contractor has been in business. Check for references of both new and old customers and talk to them. Drive by the contractor's place of business and residence too. Before signing any contract, bring the papers to an attorney to review. Ask questions. Then after hiring the contractor, hire a home inspector to play Columbo for you! Have the home inspector visit the home site with you to see that cheaper materials aren't being substituted or that other corners aren't being cut. A bit of extra footwork may help prevent your dream home from haunting you later!

CREEPY CARPET

The real estate market had slowed to a crawl when I listed Mr. Clark's home. Mr. Clark was a nice man in his sixties, a round, red-faced fellow, full of duty and devotion to his two dogs. But he was also a slob. Mr. Clark cared more about the comfort of his pets than cleaning, and as a result, the entire house smelled like a wet dog. In fact, his carpet looked dirtier than the floor at Muley's auto-body shop. It really needed to be changed. So Mr. Clark asked me the age-old question.

"Should I change the carpet or should I offer a carpet allowance?"

"Umm. Can you afford to change the carpet?" I asked him.

"Yes."

"Then I suggest that you change the carpet."

Nine times out of ten, after I say this, I'll hear the same reply as the one uttered by Mr. Clark.

"But I'm afraid that the new buyers aren't going to like the color I might choose," Mr. Clark whined. "Besides, that means I'll have to move all my things out of the rooms and that's such a hassle. What if I give a carpet allowance so the buyer can have their own choice of color? Wouldn't that be much better?"

It sounds logical, doesn't it? The problem is, homes aren't sold by logic. Emotion sells houses. So even though I got a book of carpet samples and brought it to Mr. Clark's house. I figured that buyers could see and feel the color samples that would be offered. But that idea didn't work.

After one month had passed by, and we'd gotten no offers, I made another suggestion to Mr. Clark about the carpet.

"How about getting the carpet professionally cleaned? Could you handle that?"

"Yes, I suppose I could do that."

But Mr. Clark didn't do a thing. In hindsight, he probably figured that the house might smell even worse— if that was possible.

Now here's why TV's Detective Columbo would make a great salesperson. Or at least a better salesperson than me. Because on television, Detective Columbo hounds the suspect and keeps nagging him or her about trivial details. He shows up unexpectedly at their place of work and their home. I could just imagine Columbo bagging on Mr. Clark: "When did you say you would be cleaning the carpet, Mr. Clark?"

Three months later, I received a contract on Mr. Clark's house in which the buyer asked for a $6,000 closing cost allowance. Mr. Clark agreed to this offer. Unfortunately, when the appraiser came out, the house reeked like three wet dogs, so she wrote on her appraisal report that the house needed new carpeting. In order to close escrow, Mr. Clark would have to put in new carpet *plus* pay the $6,000 for the buyer's closing costs. He didn't want to pay for both items, so the deal fell apart. A few days later, Mr. Clark called me and asked, "Do you know of anyone who can install new carpet?"

"Let's try Home Depot," I suggested.

Guess what happened after Mr. Clark put the carpet purchase on his credit card? Three days after Home Depot installed the new carpet, Mr. Clark's house sold. The new buyers didn't care that Mr. Clark had picked a carpet with a forest green color. In fact, the buyers allowed their little girl to crawl on the carpet and find "treasures" on the floor, and put them in her mouth. But there's no way they would ever have allowed her to even sit on Mr. Clark's old dirty carpet!

BOB'S BOTTOMLINE Suppose you and I play Columbo for just a minute by answering this question: Why install new carpet if you can afford to do so?

1. The scent of new carpet works emotional magic on most buyers. In contrast, the smell of old, stinky carpet is basically the kiss of death.
2. If the buyer needs to use the carpet allowance money for his closing costs, the lender may require new carpet to be installed as a condition of funding the loan. So you may end up paying for new carpet as well as the buyers' closing costs!
3. Small children and their moms love new carpet!

Do you see how playing Columbo in a real estate transaction can benefit you?

Lesson Two Final Comments

In real estate, it often helps to do a little extra investigative work. When buying or selling, don't be afraid to ask questions and check the references of anyone before you hire them. This includes realtors, attorneys, builders and home inspectors. Realize that buyers will also play Columbo, so when selling, put away valuables, thin-out possessions, and hide any embarrassing secrets!

SHORT SALES
CAN TURN SOUR

A BLONDE AND a brunette rented an airplane and after flying around for about an hour, the brunette said, "It's getting late. We'd better head back to the airport while it's still daylight." So the blonde returned to the airport and landed the plane, causing a loud screeching of tires. After they both had safely alighted, the blonde looked around the airfield.

"Wow," exclaimed the blonde. "Now that was a short runway!"

"Yes," the brunette admitted, "but look how wide it is!"

Some people, both blondes and brunettes may be unfamiliar with the term "short-sale," so let's start by defining the term. A short-sale is when a bank reduces the principal balance to allow a house to be sold. In a short-sale, for example, a person could owe $200,000 to the bank and the lender will waive $40,000 to allow the house to sell for $160,000. In addition, the lender will not pursue the borrower or take them to court to recover the waived money.

Why does a bank do this? Usually the borrower has a hardship, can't continue to make his or her monthly house payments, and needs to sell. In addition, the lender often has mortgage insurance to cover the loss, so the lender uses the insurance to pay the shortage and sells the house. This allows the borrower with the hardship to move on with his or her life. For a lending bank, cutting off nonproductive loans makes the bank's books look better, keeps the shareholders happy, and promotes a higher stock price. It's a win-win situation for everybody.

The term short-sale is also called a "short-pay"or "short pay-off" and the terms can be used interchangeably.

Now short-sales can happen in hot markets as well as cold markets. But generally you see more of them during a slow market when people are "upside down" in their properties. When someone is upside down, it means that he or she owes more to the bank than what his or her house is actually worth. I've had both good and bad experiences with short-sales. They can work out well for some people in some situations, but as you'll see, for others they can also turn into sales from hell. Which is why it's important to remember some tips concerning short-sales.

JURY DUTY

When I first met Dave and Marissa Yates, they had already suffered a string of bad luck. Mr. Yates was out of a job after surviving years of layoffs, and he and his wife had rented an apartment. They owned a house on Rotunda Road that had suffered significant earthquake damage and was unsafe to live in. However, they still owed $250,000 to the bank, and to make matters worse, their insurance company had refused to cover their claim.

The Yateses couldn't afford to make payments on a house that was unsafe to occupy plus pay for an apartment rental. They badly wanted to get rid of the house, so I suggested that they consider doing a short-pay—or short-sale on the property.

Even though the Yateses owed $250,000 to their lender, similar properties had only been selling for $215,000, so we listed their house for $205,000, subject to a bank-approved short-pay.

We submitted the Yateses' short-pay package to the lender so that the Loss Mitigation Department could get a head start in case we received an offer. Sure enough, one week later, a buyer offered $200,000, so we sent the contract to the lender in Chicago for their approval.

Four weeks went by without an answer. Then six weeks. Because the purchaser was pressed for time I showed him another property that he liked and wrote a contract on it that was accepted. In the meanwhile, an agent from XYZ Realty wrote an offer on the Yateses' property for $202,000, so we had a replacement offer tied up and waiting in the wings. We just needed to get the lender's approval.

About every three days my office faxed a letter to the lender in Chicago requesting a response. Ten weeks later, we finally received word back from the lender. Here's what had happened. Apparently, the manager in charge of handling the short-sales for the bank had been out on jury duty for twelve weeks. That's right, jury duty! Since nobody else in that office knew how to handle short-pays, she never processed the Yateses' transaction.

"Do the buyers still wish to proceed on this transaction?" she asked me.

Even though our initial buyer had already found another home, our poor sellers were dying to sell. So an idea came to me that if the bank could grant us an approval, maybe we could get the new XYZ Realty offer accepted by the bank. So I told a white lie.

"Yes, these buyers still want to pursue this transaction," I said.

"Your buyers are very patient. Either that or the property is undervalued. I'd better get another broker price opinion on this property before I give you an answer."

So she burned another week updating her broker price opinion.

Approximately thirteen weeks after we submitted our original paperwork, we finally got an answer.

Do you know what the short-sale lender told us? "Our records indicate that we sold this loan to another bank a few weeks ago. You'll have to start the short-sale process all over with that new lender."

Because of their frustration waiting for the short-pay approval, the Yateses allowed their home to go to a foreclosure sale. Our faxed cover-sheets and the letters we had written for theYateses helped prove it wasn't my company's fault, and a few years later, they purchased another home from my firm.

BOB'S BOTTOMLINE When dealing with short-sales, expect time delays. Now some people may tell you to call the lender constantly and be a "squeaky wheel," however I've found that it doesn't pay to a pest. It's better to send the lender an e-mail or a fax. Why? The faxed pages have to be filed by a clerk, and eventually after enough faxes are sent, the clerk needs to put your file at the top of the stack to more readily file the faxed pages. If you are dealing with a government loan, however I've found that an e-mail works better than a fax.

CONTINGENCY CLAUSES

John and Tracy Baltz found an ad in the paper that read, "Lakefront Property Only $145,000." Excited, they called Jimmy Wessell, the listing agent to see if the ad was a misprint. "No, the ad is correct," gushed Jimmy. "Come on down and let's write it up!"

The Baltzes put the city in their rear-view mirror and showed up at the lakefront real estate office with a pre-approval letter from their lender in hand. Jimmy, the listing agent, wrote the contract "subject to lender's approval of a short-sale." At that time, Tracy questioned the listing agent. "What does that mean? Subject to a short-sale?"

"Even though the listed price is $145,000, the sellers owe $225,000 to the bank," explained Jimmy. "Let's write up the offer for $145,000 and see what happens. We should have an answer for you in thirty days."

Three months later, John and Tracy still hadn't received an answer from the lender on the short-pay. In the meantime, a new listing came on the market for $160,000 in a better location on the lake that was not subject to a short-pay. John and Tracy wanted to purchase this other home but, like most people, they were curious to see if the bank would accept their offer for $145,000 for the first property. The next day, Tracy asked Jimmy, "Have you received offers from any other buyers on the short-pay lakefront property?"

"Yes, I've now got seven," replied Jimmy.

Realizing that the bank would probably take a higher offer than theirs, John and Tracy pointed out to Jimmy that his contract contained a contingency that the bank could accept any offer prior to acceptance of the short-pay. So they canceled their offer with Jimmy and then used another real estate agent to write an offer on the other lakefront home listed for $160,000.

BOB'S BOTTOMLINE Most short-sales contain a contingency that allows the bank to accept a better offer prior to short-pay approval because the time frame for receiving a response from a bank can be approximately two to four weeks or longer in some cases. This is where short-sales can be tricky. So when purchasing a short-sale, be sure to include some kind of escape clause in the purchase contract. For example, "In the event the seller does not receive approval by the short-sale lender(s) by June 14, buyer may, at buyer's option, cancel this contract without penalty."

INSPECTION BLUES

John Devine liked to wear a black shirt, cowboy hat, boots and blue jeans. He was interested in purchasing horse property and found a ranch that was being sold "subject to and contingent upon the approval of the short-sale lender." John wrote a full-price offer on the property that was listed for $300,000. This buyer paid for a home inspection, well test, and he even hired a surveyor to locate the property corners.

The home inspector found some defective items that the seller agreed to fix, and approximately five days prior to the closing, John conducted a final walk-through inspection. At this time, he discovered that the seller had not fixed any of the agreed upon items.

"What's going on?" John asked Nigel, the listing agent. "I paid full price for this property and have waited three months to get this short-sale approved. I'm only asking that the seller fix a few items. Why hasn't the seller fixed them?"

"The deal is off," said Nigel. "Even though the bank has approved the short-sale, the seller has suddenly decided not to go through with it."

"What?" John exclaimed. "He can't do that, can he?"

"You may wish to speak to an attorney. You could sue the seller for breach of contract and specific performance but that might not get you very far. Apparently, the seller has no money and has just now realized that under a short-sale he will have to pay the IRS about sixteen thousand dollars in taxes. Therefore, he's going to stay in the house until the lender forecloses on the loan."

BOB'S BOTTOMLINE Buyer beware. Many sellers do not realize that short-sales do involve paying taxes to the IRS. Sometimes when sellers realize how much it will cost them, they bail out. Also, purchasing a property subject to the approval of a short-sale lender does involve risk. As a buyer, you may spend money on inspecting the property plus the costs of the appraisal and the credit report only to have the seller back out at the last minute. The buyer's recourse then is to mediate, arbitrate or sue, and to request that the seller pay the buyer's damages based on the out-of-pocket expenses that he or she has incurred.

CAN YOU SPARE A DIME?

Randy Hunt was a short, athletic-looking man who dressed like a high school prep student. His father had left him with a large inheritance and Randy regularly attended the trust deed auctions that were held once every two weeks on the steps of the county courthouse. One day, Randy was going to bid on a property that had two loans against it for a total of $165,000. This property was actually only worth $145,000.

Why should Randy bid on this house?

Well, Randy had played Columbo, and he discovered an error in the deed. The legal description for the first trust deed referred to another property. Therefore, the first loan of $125,000 was NOT secured by the subject property on the auction—but a different property altogether. That meant that there was only one lien—the second trust deed for $40,000 against the property!

The second trust deed holder was having the foreclosure sale and didn't realize the mistake. In fact, he thought that his second trust deed was valueless and would be extinguished by the first trust deed holder, so he was willing to take anything for it. Randy showed up at the court house with three cashier's checks (for $2,000, $10,000, and $40,000) in case he got into a bidding war with other investors who may have also discovered the mistake.

To Randy's surprise, there was only one other person attending the auction— a homeless man missing several teeth who usually sat on the steps of the courthouse with a bucket full of loose change and a handwritten cardboard sign that read "Will work for food."

The Court Administrator opened the auction by announcing,

"Who will give me an opening bid?" Before Randy could raise his hand, the homeless man sat up and joked, "I'll give you one dollar for it."

"Okay, one dollar once," said the Administrator, and Randy couldn't believe his ears. "One dollar twice," announced the administrator.

"Wait. One dollar and two cents," Randy interjected.

"One dollar and four cents," returned the homeless man.

"A dollar and six cents," replied Randy.

On and on the bidding went until the Court Administrator said, "One dollar and seventeen cents, twice..."

"Ah shucks. You can have it!" laughed the homeless man.

The Administrator announced, "Sold, for one dollar and seventeen cents to the gentleman with the red necktie. I need your cash please."

Then, to Randy's horror, he discovered that he didn't have one dollar and seventeen cents! He had all those cashier's checks in his fanny pack along with a slew of twenty dollar bills in his wallet but nothing smaller.

The administrator repeated, "I need exact change, please."

Thinking quickly, Randy asked the homeless guy, "Look dude, can I give you twenty dollars in exchange for a dollar and seventeen cents?"

The homeless guy sent Randy a toothless smile. "Anytime." And that's how Randy purchased a home in the year 2001 for eighteen dollars and eighty-three cents.

$20–$1.17 = $18.83

One day after the auction, Randy purchased a title insurance policy against the property. One month later, after the title insurance policy was in place, Randy fixed up the house and then sold it for $135,000.

BOB'S BOTTOMLINE This story doesn't involve a short-sale but the lesson to learn is the part about quickly getting a title insurance policy. Sometimes, if one cannot get a title insurance policy, the property that is purchased can become a nightmare that can come back to haunt a new owner later on down the road as you'll see in the next story.

TAX SALE FROM HELL

Jim Curtis was a friendly red-haired man who purchased a vacant lot at a tax auction. Jim paid $1,527 for the property which was one dollar more than the old taxes that were owed by the previous owner.

Jim needed money badly. He showed the deed from the tax sale to his friend Fred Kimble and asked Fred if he could borrow $15,000 against his new property. Fred knew that the vacant land was worth at least $50,000 and figured that if Jim didn't make his payments, then the land would be his.

Jim promised to pay Fred the $15,000 and he signed a note secured by a deed of trust which was recorded with the county against his new property. However, this was a private transaction between two individuals. The forms they used were purchased at an Office Max store. No title insurance was purchased and no escrow office was ever involved. No attorney reviewed the title or any of the documents.

One year later, Jim received a strange letter from a man claiming to be the true owner of the vacant land. This man claimed that the county made a mistake and that he did indeed pay up his back taxes prior to the tax redemption period. Therefore the deed issued to Jim was worthless, as title never transferred. Jim called the County Tax Assessor who told Jim that the man was correct. The ownership of the property was never transferred to Jim Curtis because the county was slow in registering the fact that the true owner had paid his taxes.

Now the true owner told Jim, "I'm in the process of selling the property for $50,000 and if your buddy Fred Kimble doesn't remove his deed from the property, he will be sued for three times the amount of the buyer's offer, or $150,000."

BOB'S BOTTOMLINE Many tax authorities, including the IRS, are unreliable for maintaining accurate records. So before buying a property and selling it quickly, or borrowing against it, purchase title insurance. In a similar note, some states have mortgages with various redemption periods. For example, a homeowner may have up to one year and a day to make up their back payments and redeem the title, so make certain the time limit for redemption has expired before trying to sell, encumber, or move into the property.

DEATH & TAXES

Kevin and Inga Sorenson had refinanced their home and were later told by a real estate agent that they would NOT be good candidates for a short-sale. Even though Kevin had lost his job and couldn't make his house payments, the agent told them that their lender might still be able to collect a "deficiency judgment" against them if they tried to do a short-sale. Why? Because the Sorensons had refinanced their loan. In California, a borrower who takes out a purchase loan and then later refinances may find themselves in an awkward situation if attempting to do a short-sale. Why? Because the new loan company may be able to go to court and collect a judgment against the borrower for the unpaid debt. To avoid having to pay the judgment, some borrowers turn to third parties, such as Boston Infinity, a short-sale assistance company.

One day, Kevin heard an ad on the radio for a company called Boston Infinity. The ad said that Boston Infinity would handle a short-sale transaction on behalf of *any* seller.

Kevin called the company and asked about his situation. He spoke with a salesperson on the phone who assured him that Boston Infinity had processed thousands of similar short-pay requests. "We work differently than a normal short-sale," claimed the Boston Infinity salesperson. "Here's how we work. You'll sign a quickclaim deed to our company which transfers the ownership of your property to our corporation. That moves the debt liability to our corporation, so you will pay no taxes to the IRS, plus you will be free from all other debt liabilities."

Taking the salesperson at his word, Kevin sent in $895 dollars to Boston Infinity for the short-sale kit. He then completed the paperwork and quitclaimed his property to Boston Infinity. Afterwards, Kevin and Inga moved to Oregon feeling like they had done the right thing.

Two years later, however, the Sorensons received a letter from the IRS demanding payment on the debt that was waived, plus penalties on the discharged debt.

BOB'S BOTTOMLINE Before agreeing to a third-party short-sale, check with your tax advisor and get his or her advice in writing to see if the situation will work for you. Normally when a bank discharges debt, it will give you a 1099, and the IRS will still consider it taxable income regardless of what happens to the title. In other words, you may be able to avoid a deficiency judgment from a creditor by quitclaiming to a corporation, but you'll still need to pay the Internal Revenue Service.

SHORT SALE SUCCESS

Juan and Aracelli Trujillo were pre-approved to buy a home. They saw an ad in the newspaper advertising a house for sale for $65,000. They were shown the house by their agent Maria who wrote an offer for $55,000 with the seller paying $3,000 towards the buyer's closing costs, subject to the approval of the seller's short-sale lender.

Kathy, the listing agent was on the ball. She had sent out the necessary information to the short-sale lender who then only needed a written contract from a willing buyer in order to grant the short-sale approval. Because

Kathy hadn't received any other bids on the property, the short-sale lender approved the offer from Juan and Aracelli for $55,000 and agreed to pay $3,000 for their closing costs.

The lender faxed his approval in three days and signed a release form to reduce the amount of the deed so that the property could close escrow.

BOB'S BOTTOMLINE Not all buyers experience failure at purchasing a short-sale. The key to a successful transaction is to have an experienced short-sale lender, a seller who gathers the required information promptly, and a pre-approved buyer. The failure of a bank to sign the release, a buyer who is not approved, and a seller who does not qualify for the short-sale can all kill the deal.

COLUMBO TIME!

Dana Roswell, a seller with large quiet eyes, was caught between a rock and a hard spot. Her house was appraised for $200,000, but she couldn't make her house payments because of an injury at her job. Yet Dana couldn't sell her home either because she owed $195,000 to the bank. I suggested a short-sale. We listed Dana's home for $187,000 and found a buyer who was willing to pay $185,000.

In this case, we needed the bank to eat the shortage of $23,000. Where did the $23,000 come from?

Dana owes $195,000
Sales price: $185,000
Difference: $10,000
Plus Dana's closing costs: $13,000
$10,000 + $13,000 = $23,000 total.

As an agent, I disclosed the following to Dana:

1. The IRS would look at the $23,000 of discharged debt as taxable income. At the end of the year, Dana would need to pay about $5,000 in taxes on the $23,000 that was waived by the lender. However, Dana was already filing for bankruptcy so she could close escrow on the short-sale first, and then walk into the bankruptcy court to make the IRS debt part of her bankruptcy.

   Currently, if you can prove to the IRS that you are insolvent, you don't have to pay taxes on the discharged debt (IRS Code 108). Check with your tax advisor first before doing so, as bankruptcy laws periodically change.

2. I also informed Dana that the short-sale would leave a black mark on her credit rating. However, it would not be as damaging as a full foreclosure, in which the lender would seize Dana's home outright for nonpayment of the mortgage. Still it would show up—as would her bankruptcy.

Back to Dana's short-sale transaction. Dana had a first trust deed for $150,000 and a second trust deed for $45,000. So either one of the two banks could have possibly reduced what was owed in order for the short-sale to go through.

I called the first lender who was owed $150,000 to start negotiations. "Would you consider waiving $23,000 so that my client can sell her home?"

"No way," the bank's short-sale specialist told me. "This house is worth $195,000. Once we foreclose on our note, it automatically extinguishes the second lien for $45,000. Therefore, we will resell the property and make a tidy profit."

I told Dana what the first lender had said. Then I opened my big mouth. I said, "Dana, I am almost one-hundred percent certain that the bank holding the second trust deed will agree to reduce the amount of their forty-five thousand dollar note by twenty-three thousand dollars. Why? Because the second trust deed holder will lose the entire forty-five thousand if the first holder forecloses."

But when I talked to the vice-president of the second bank, he told me, "Go jump in a lake, Bob. There's no way we're going to help out this borrower." I suggested to him, "Isn't getting something better than losing everything?"

I reminded him, "If the holder of the first trust deed forecloses, you, as the second trust deed holder will lose everything. Isn't $22,000 better than getting nothing?"

2nd Bank is owed: $45,000
Less shortage: $23,000
Balance: $22,000

The Vice-President told me, "We won't lose a penny on this deal. In fact, I'll probably get promoted."

Click.

The wheels in my head started to turn. This bank official seemed pretty cocky. The way he boasted about getting promoted reminded me that it was time to play Columbo and do some more research.

After all, why would he make such a statement?

I ordered a property profile on the house from a title company and requested to see copies of both deeds that had been recorded on the property. That's when I discovered *why* the bank Vice-President sounded so confident.

Originally, Dana had purchased the house with a loan that had a fixed interest rate for only five years. After five years, there was a two month "window period" where Dana could refinance. However, if she didn't refinance the loan, it would become a variable rate loan. While refinancing this first loan, Dana had also taken out a second loan for home repairs.

Here's what happened. The same escrow company processed the paperwork on both loans. Apparently, the "second" loan of $45,000 got recorded *before* the "first" loan for $150,000!

What this means to you is that the $45,000 loan became the first trust deed. The loan for $150,000 became the second trust deed!

Like my client Randy who had purchased the house for $18.83, the Vice-President of the second loan had planned to ace out the $150,000 loan and then resell Dana's property for a huge profit. That's why he could see himself getting promoted.

Unfortunately for the Vice-President of the $45,000 loan, however, the bank that was owed $150,000 received a mysterious telephone call from a real estate agent who sounded a little like Columbo. He asked the short-sale specialist a dumb question. He asked, "Just one more thing, sir. Could you fax me a document that proves that your loan was recorded before the loan of $45,000?"

"You don't give up, do you?" laughed the short-sale specialist. "No problem."

Then a funny thing happened in this transaction. My escrow officer called me on the phone and she sounded amazed. She said, "Bob, you won't believe what just happened. We got a faxed approval today on your short-sale. The bank that was owed $150,000 suddenly agreed to waive the $23,000."

"They did?" I said, trying to sound equally surprised.

"Yes! Isn't that amazing?"

BOB'S BOTTOMLINE Columbo strikes again.

UNPLEASANT PARTNERS

Philip Martin purchased a triplex with a partner, Jake Adams, during the high time of the real estate market. Later, there was a septic tank problem that would cost at least $6,000 to fix, and the tenants refused to pay their rent until the gross smell went away and the plumbing got fixed. Because the property value had gone down, the two partners were upside down in the property. Jake didn't wish to contribute any money to repair it, but Philip wanted to have it fixed so that his credit wouldn't be damaged.

"We are partners, Jake. We agreed to split the costs fifty-fifty."

"Nope. I'm not going to sink one more nickel into this money pit," Jake declared.

Philip didn't think that was fair. "Wait, we're both in this together, Jake. Why should I have to foot the entire repair bill?"

"You don't," said Jake. "In fact, I could care less what you want to do. I hope I never see your ugly face again. I want out of this partnership."

"Look, I know you're angry with me, but we can't let the house slide into foreclosure. It's going to ruin both our credit. Let's sell this house and go our separate ways."

So rather than fix the house, Phil and Jake listed the property with Jillian Hernandez and dissolved their business partnership.

They had originally purchased the property for $175,000. The current value was $135,000, less $10,000 in commissions and costs. Jillian suggested that they list the property for $133,000, subject to a lender-approved short-pay.

"Do you think the lender will approve the short-pay?" Phil asked Jillian.

"This property was insured by Freddie Mac, so there's a good chance for a short-sale," she told Phil.

Some background. Freddie Mac is a stockholder-owned corporation that provides funds to mortgage lenders. Freddie Mac purchases mortgages from lenders and packages them into securities that are sold to investors on the New York Stock Exchange. Visit their Web site at www.freddiemac.com for more information.

Three weeks after sending in all the paperwork required in the short-sale package, Jill received a fax letter from Freddie Mac stating that they would approve a short-sale offer with one condition. Separately, both Philip and Jake must agree to pay Freddie Mac $3,000 after the close of escrow.

Jill's heart sank to her stomach. She knew that both Jake and Phil were adamant about not spending one more dollar on this property. Especially Jake. Making payments to Freddie Mac after the property had already closed escrow did not seem like a winning proposition, but she relayed the information to the two business partners.

To her surprise, however, even though Jake and Philip could not agree to pay $6,000 to repair the plumbing problem, they both agreed to sign a note to Freddie Mac. They would make monthly payments with no interest for a three-year period or until the loans of $3,000 had been repaid.

BOB'S BOTTOMLINE The three "D's" of selling real estate are Death, Divorce and Dissolution of a business partnership. In many dissolving business partnerships, many people would rather cut their losses and pay to save their credit than continue sinking money into a losing investment.

Lesson Three Final Comments

An approved lender short-sale allows people with hardships to sell properties for less than what is owed against them. Oftentimes, there are time delays as well as certain conditions for approval and risks for purchasers. The terms and conditions for short-pays on government loans may be different than conventional loans. Sellers are advised to seek competent tax and legal counsel.

Lesson 4

LEASE OPTIONS

CAN BE LOUSY

A MAN RUSHES INTO his house and yells to his wife, "Monica, pack up your things, I just won the California lottery!"

Overjoyed, Monica says, "Shall I pack for warm weather or cold?"

The man responds, "I don't care. Just get all your stuff out of the house by noon!"

I mention this joke because sometimes people will use a lease option to buy or sell a home and they feel higher than a kite. It's like they've won the state lottery. Then a few months later, the buyer or seller begins to feel like the wife being asked to pack up her things. Why? Because sometimes a lease option can turn ugly.

In this chapter, the main lesson to be learned is that sellers usually do lease options when they have no other choice. Most lease options also favor the seller and allow the seller to charge a higher than market rent. So if you are a buyer and wish to purchase a home using a lease option, proceed with caution.

THE HAUNTED HOUSE

Jim Morrow wished to purchase a property, but he didn't have a large down payment and his credit score was low. In addition, Jim felt intimidated by banks. Sitting down and talking to a lender felt as forced as the contestant interviews on TV's *Jeopardy*.

"Jim, your credit is not half bad," said a lender referred by a friend. "If you continue to make timely payments on your credit cards, by next year, your credit score will be good enough to purchase a home."

"What do you suggest I do in the meantime?" Jim asked.

"Find a lease option. One where you pay $3,000 for the option money—to lock the price in today. And $1,300 a month, with $300 going towards the purchase, and $1,000 as the fair market rental."

"People will do that?"

"Yes."

Jim scoured the newspaper, and as luck would have it, he spied an ad that read, "Lease Option, $3,000 down, $1,300 per month."

Jim visited the owner, a man named Bill who seemed like a nice old fellow. Bill was tall and wore a cashmere sweater. "This lease option seems almost too good to be true," said Jim. "Why are you selling the house in this manner?"

"Well, I'll be honest with you," replied the old man. "This house belonged to my brother-in-law who hanged himself in the garage. The word spread through the town that this house is haunted, and that's why I'm having a problem selling it. I thought a lease option might work."

"I see," said Jim. "Mind if I think things over tonight?"

"No problem," said Bill. "You're not afraid, are you?"

"Not really," said Jim. "I'm more afraid of living people than the dead, actually."

"That's a good attitude!"

"I'll call you tomorrow morning at nine o'clock," Jim promised.

"Excellent."

You can probably guess what happened next.

Jim called the next day at nine in the morning and a woman answered the phone. She said, "You talked to Bill about the house yesterday and he told you to call today? But that's impossible."

"Why?"

"Because Bill sold the house at ten o'clock last night. I don't see why he would ask you to call this morning."

"I met with him at five o'clock, ma'am."

"Oh, then that explains it."

BOB'S BOTTOMLINE Finding a good lease option is sometimes as rare as finding someone smarter than Albert Einstein and more popular than Oprah Winfrey. If the lease option meets your terms and conditions, act quickly or you may be haunted by its memory!

RECORDING REGRETS

Joe and Sara Reynolds purchased their home with an option to buy from Arnie. Arnie was one of those people who bathe once every other year. In a voice that resembled Oscar the Grouch, Arnie told Joe, "Just to be safe, I want to record the option with the County Recorder's office." Then three months later, after Joe and Sara had comfortably settled into their new home, they received a letter from Arnie

"Dear Mr. and Mrs. Reynolds," read the letter. "I regret to inform you that my bank has found out about our recent transaction and considers our lease option agreement an attempt to transfer title without their consent. They are now calling my loan due and payable. Therefore, I will need you to either: (1) close escrow in fifteen days or (2) move out of the house. If you act promptly, I will refund your entire $5,000 option money, but only on the condition that you move out of the premises immediately. I need to sell the property to a party who can close escrow quickly. Obviously, if you can close escrow quickly, I'll sell the property to you. Arnie"

Joe and Sara decided that it would be better to move out and get their money refunded than to lose everything and still have to move.

BOB'S BOTTOMLINE

Beware of recording a lease option or option to purchase. Many times, the lender will call the loan due and payable, and in California, the property may be reassessed for higher taxes.

A HAPPY TALE

Donald Martin was a big man with a problem bigger than Shaquille O'Neal. He couldn't sell his house. He had it on the market for five months without receiving a single offer! Donald felt like he was at the end of his rope. He didn't really want to rent out the property because he had upgraded the carpets to sell the home, but now he was faced with that prospect. Donald's last rental experience had been a nightmare.

"What should I do?" Donald asked his real estate agent Barbara. "I've been transferred to Detroit. I've got to get my kids in school. My job starts next week, and to top it off, my wife is pregnant!"

"Why not try a lease option?" Barbara suggested.

"Won't the bank call the note due and payable?" Donald asked.

"There's a chance of that if the option is recorded," Barbara explained. "But usually, the bank doesn't care who is making the payments, just as long as they get their money."

"Well, I can't afford to keep making double payments. I've been doing that for three months now and it's killing me."

"Why not give a lease option a try?"

"OK. Let's try it," Donald decided. "But dot every I and cross every T so that the buyer can't get out of this deal."

BOB'S BOTTOMLINE Lease options sometimes work well as a last resort—if a seller needs to sell and has the funds to make a payment just in case the optionee's payment arrives late. If you're a buyer though, beware! Nationwide, only 24% of optionees end up purchasing the property at the end of the term, so some sellers take a predatory approach. They'll choose an unsophisticated buyer who has no hope of ever qualifying for a home loan in the future. The sophisticated seller can receive higher-than-market rent for his option, plus take the option money up front, as well as gain time to ride out a slow market. Later the seller will sell the house for a higher price when the market improves. So don't forget: lease options favor the seller.

TRANSFER CLAUSE

Randy Hunt approached me with a big smile on his face and a lease option agreement in his hand.

"Can you believe this deal?" he laughed. "I'm buying a house with a lease option!"

"Why would you want to do that?" I said aloud. "You're worth a million dollars. Why buy a property via a lease option?"

Randy grinned. "Dude, check this out. See this clause that reads, 'Assignment'? I checked this tiny box and the seller put his initials right beside it. This box gives me the right to 'assign' or 'transfer' the lease option to anyone I want without having to send the new buyer's credit or financial information to the seller. The seller insisted I give him a copy of my credit report, so I did. Big deal. I have stellar credit. But now I can turn around and sell this lease option to any loser who has twenty grand and the seller can't ask to check their credit!"

Sure enough, two days later, Randy placed an ad in the local newspaper that shouted: "Take over payments! Only $25,000 down! No qualifying!"

He sold this lease option in five days.

BOB'S BOTTOMLINE Sellers who sell "by owner" or who transfer property via lease option "by owner" should remember that it's a good idea to fax the papers to a lawyer for his or her approval before signing them. If you can't afford a lawyer, fax them to a real estate agent you trust. Offer to pay for their time. Remember, there are many sophisticated buyers who will take advantage of unsophisticated sellers, and visa versa.

HERE COMES THE JUDGE!

Margaret and Thomas Jersey gave $3,000 to Steve Barnes as option money to purchase Steve's home in three years. In addition, Steve also had the Jerseys sign a one-year rental agreement, but no mention was made of a rental deposit in that contract.

Two months before the option to purchase expired, the

Jerseys wrote to Steve to tell him that they would be moving out of the house by the 30th of April.

"Great," said Steve to a friend. "I get to keep the $3,000 option money given to me by Margaret and Thomas Jersey."

By May 1st, Steve signed a new option agreement with another couple, and he collected another $3,000. Then on June 1st, Steve was surprised to find a letter addressed to him from Margaret and Thomas.

"Dear Steve," read the letter. "According to our rental contract, we were supposed to receive an itemized letter regarding our security deposit after we moved out. You never sent us that letter and we would now like to you to return our entire security deposit of $3,000, or we will take you to small claims court."

"Security deposit?" Steve said to his friend, sounding surprised. "What are they talking about? The three thousand dollars was option money not a security deposit for a rental. They left prior to the end of the contract! They signed an option to purchase my house, but they reneged, so I get to keep their $3,000 option money. That's how it works!"

At the small claims court hearing, Steve showed his written paperwork to the judge, who asked Steve if it was true that he never sent the Jerseys an itemized accounting letter for their security deposit.

"Yes it's true, your honor," said Steve, "But I have an explanation. The Jerseys signed an option to buy my house. Before you are the two agreements."

"I don't see any security deposit for this rental contract," stated the judge. "You will receive my written response by mail."

Can you guess what happened next?

Steve lost the case. The California judge ruled in favor of the Jerseys and remanded Steve to refund the full $3,000 to Margaret and Thomas.

BOB'S BOTTOMLINE No buyer truly wishes to lose his or her option money. And, if not stated in the rental contract, most buyers will do their best to convince a judge that the option money acted as a rental deposit. So if you offer an option to purchase, be careful not to confuse the option money with the rental deposit. You may wish to clarify the funds received as the diagram below and have the optionee(s) approve the agreement by placing their initials or signature(s) in the appropriate box. Or better yet, take a security deposit!

Security Deposit ____________	0
Rent from 12/1–12/31 ____________	$850
Option Money ____________	$3,000
Optionor (initial/date) ____________	*Steve Barnes*
Optionee (initial/date) ____________	*Thomas Jersey*

The box above would have clarified that there was not a rental deposit and that all of the $3,000 was credited towards the option. However, since the optionee gave a proper 60 day notice and then left the house prior to exercising their option, Steve should still have sent an itemized accounting about the rental deposit within the allotted time period. In California, it is two weeks for an unfurnished place and three weeks if it is furnished.

CHECK PLEASE!

Jill and Terry Parks were aware that only 24% of all buyers who purchase a home using a lease option agreement actually complete the transaction. Nevertheless, they agreed to enter into a lease option agreement. They gave $10,000 in the form of a personal check to Larry Diaz for their option consideration money.

Two years later, Jill and Terry exercised their option on the property and opened escrow.

"Your loan is approved subject to one condition," said their mortgage broker.

"What's the condition?"

"We need to see a copy of the $10,000 personal check that you gave to Mr. Diaz."

Terry called her bank to get a copy of the check, however the bank couldn't find it. The seller offered to show proof that $10,000 was deposited in his account two years ago, but the lender wouldn't accept that evidence as proof.

"The only way the bank will make this loan now is if Mr. Diaz puts $10,000 into escrow. That way, we know this wasn't a fraudulent transaction," said the mortgage broker.

Fortunately, Larry had $10,000 that he could wire to escrow, and Jill and Terry's house closed successfully.

BOB'S

BOTTOMLINE To avoid future problems, never use a personal check for the option money. Always pay with a cashier's check. Then make a copy of the cashier's check and keep it in a file with the rest of your paperwork!

INSURANCE WOES

Cindy and Steve Slaynick sold their townhome to Mary Clapper via a lease option. Mary was a cool, confident woman with a surprising intellect. Fully expecting that she would purchase this home during the first three years, Mary gave $10,000 to the Slaynicks for the option money.

Two months later, a pipe in the wall between the neighbor's and Mary's townhouse burst, and water flooded the family room. The water ruined the carpet and some of Mary's furnishings.

Mary called Cindy and Steve. "I need somebody to get here fast," she told them.

"We'll do our best," Steve responded. "However, we're waiting for the homeowner association's insurance company to call us."

The water damage company arrived with fans, but the carpet was already completely ruined. It was dried with the fans and then removed. In addition, six inches of drywall was cut from the bottom of each wall in the family room.

Eventually, the water damage was repaired and things got back to normal.

In the summer, however, Mary discovered that the air conditioner didn't work. This item wasn't covered by the homeowner insurance. Since Mary wasn't the owner of record, she didn't wish to pay to repair it.

Mary called Steve and Cindy.

"I want my money back," she told Steve. "The air conditioner doesn't work and I don't have the money to fix it."

Unfortunately, Steve and Cindy didn't have her money. Anticipating that she would actually purchase the property, they had spent the $10,000 she gave them on their honeymoon! Thinking quickly, Steve remembered that he and Cindy had purchased a home warranty on the property. “Cindy, if the air conditioning isn’t working in three days, you’ll have your money back. Fair enough?”

Cindy agreed to give Steve three days to fix the air conditioning.

The next day, a repairman sent from the home warranty company stopped by Cindy’s townhouse to look at the a/c unit. Apparently, when the insurance company had installed the new carpet, someone had accidentally punched a hole in the air conditioning condenser. The home warranty company agreed to install a brand new air conditioner for Steve and Cindy. Because of his quick thinking, Steve saved the transaction and Mary later closed escrow on the property. Whew!

BOB’S BOTTOMLINE Life is often messy so splurge and purchase a home warranty policy. It costs about $350 but can be renewed at the same price each year for three years. Nowadays, just two claims against one’s normal homeowner insurance can cause an insurance company to raise their rates or decline future coverage, so a home warranty can be a real lifesaver! If you are the seller, have the bill sent to your home address so that the optionee doesn’t trash it. Remember, it’s not the problem that’s the problem, it’s how you deal with the problem!

LESSON FOUR FINAL COMMENTS

A lease option gives a right to a tenant to purchase the property under certain terms. It's usually the last resort for a seller because they have no other choice. Purchasers should be aware that the odds are stacked against them, and sellers should take care not to violate any local laws regarding landlord/tenant relationships. A lawsuit from a disgruntled optionee is always a possibility, and because most lawyers believe a bad settlement is better than a good trial, it's important to dot your "i"s and cross your "t"s.

> Nice guys do finish first. If you don't know that, then maybe you just don't know where the finish line is.
>
> —*Garry Shandling*

Daffy Definitions

Appraiser: One who compliments your house for money. Example: "Appraiser here, ma'am. Gee, this is a lovely home! And what nice taste you have! That'll be three hundred and fifty bucks, ma'am."

Attorney: An expensive lawyer.

Buyer: A person who actively solicits the help of real estate people, has no money nor the ability to raise same, and has not yet placed his present home on the market.

Cash Flow: The phenomenon of money rushing rapidly downstream in the wake of a real estate purchase.

Condominium: From the Latin word meaning "to share walls with those of lesser intelligence," it is a legal form of ownership...that involves taking a large comfortable living area, and dividing it up until each resulting space is too small for habitation, and then selling these tiny spaces for an unconscionable profit.

Co-signor: When home purchase is imminent, this is a form of endearment directed toward solvent relatives.

Foreclosure: A lender's way of teasing the unemployed.

Library: A quiet haven of refuge in which one can enjoy reading in privacy. More commonly called a bathroom.

Rent: The marvelously selfless system that allows those who don't own real estate the pleasure of paying off the mortgages of those who do.

Shingle: Thin, rectangular pieces of wood, asbestos, asphalt, tin or slate which are found in your yard after a storm.

Yard: A plot of land that surrounds a house and is designed to prevent its owner from enjoying himself on weekends.

—By Roger Reitzel in *Real Estate as a Second Language*

LESSON 5

SPEAK UP
OR PAY THE PRICE

WHEN I FIRST STARTED selling homes, I met a man named Alfred who was selling his home "by owner." I was eager to take listings, so when Alfred told me that he wanted to net $50,000 from the sale of his house, I worked up all the numbers on a calculator and showed Alfred in writing that he would net $50,000 if he listed his home with me. Alfred signed my listing agreement, and about two weeks later, another agent brought us a full-price offer. After approving the contract, I had Alfred sign a net sheet that I'd prepared. On this net sheet, I'd itemized all the costs associated with selling and had subtracted them from the sales price. Again, I estimated that Alfred would receive $50,000.

It was a good thing he signed that net sheet too, because after closing escrow, Alfred claimed that escrow had shorted him by $6,000. He'd received only $44,000 from escrow, and when he came to my office to visit me, he was not a happy camper!

I compared my net sheet with the closing statement he'd received from escrow and I noticed that escrow had charged him $6,000 for a pre-payment penalty. Alfred never told me about a prepayment penalty. In fact, he swore up and down that he didn't have one so I called escrow to verify it. Apparently, among all the papers that Alfred had signed when he originally purchased the house was a document from the bank acknowledging that Alfred would owe a prepayment penalty if he paid the loan off early. For those of you who don't know about this term, a prepayment penalty is basically a fine for paying off a loan before its maturity.

My point is that it's important to carefully check things before signing and then to speak up—especially if you don't understand what you're signing. In Alfred's case, he might have checked with his bank when I first asked him about having a prepayment penalty. Or when he purchased the home he could have asked his escrow officer, "What does this sentence mean?" Or simply, "Do I have a prepayment penalty?"

Here are some more stories that show that silence isn't always golden in real estate!

UNHAPPY WITH HARRY

Megan and Steve Freeman listed their condominium with Harry Hunter, known locally as "Harry, the Condo King." Megan and Steve were impressed at first with Harry's enthusiasm and attention to detail, but then five weeks passed by. During this time, Harry hadn't brought a single buyer to their condo.

At a dinner party one evening, a friend asked Steve: "So are you happy with Harry?"

"Not really. Harry never returns my phone messages," Steve complained. "Not even once has he called me back!"

"That's odd," said the friend. "How can he stay in business?"

"Well a lady from his office named Hillary is the one who calls me."

BOB'S BOTTOMLINE There's a sign in a local restaurant that reads, "If you like the food, tell your friends. If you don't like the food, tell the chef." In other words, if Steve is unhappy with Harry for not returning messages, Steve ought to speak his mind directly to Harry and not to the people at the party. Or even better, when first listing the home, Harry should speak up and explain to Steve in advance, "Steve, this is how I like to work. Any call you make to me will be handled by my assistant, Hillary, so don't expect me to return your calls." Harry is like most real estate agents. We won't know that we're doing something wrong unless somebody tells us. So if you're unhappy with your agent, talk directly to him or her! Don't assume that your agent and/or assistant can read your mind.

COUNTER-OFFER

Larry, a local real estate agent, met with Mr. Alonzo who wished to sell his condo. Mr. Alonzo had purchased the property through Larry during a hot real estate market. However, when Mr. Alonzo listed his house with Larry, the market suddenly turned cold. Three months passed and they didn't get even one offer. One day, Larry received a fax sent to him from an out-of-town broker. The eight-page fax was a full-price offer on Mr. Alonzo's condo! Larry showed the offer to Mr. Alonzo.

"Finally," said Mr. Alonzo. "Where do I sign?"

"Wait. I don't think you should sign this contract, sir," Larry advised him.

"Why not?"

"They have specified CBA Escrow Company," Larry noted.

"So?"

"Well, ABC Escrow is much better than CBA," Larry explained. "ABC Escrow is more objective and experienced. Plus their escrow fee is lower and I can keep a better handle on things at ABC Escrow."

Instead of speaking his mind and accepting the counter offer, Mr. Alonzo went along with Larry's direction. After all, everybody likes to save money, don't they? And Mr. Alonzo was no different than anyone else.

The truth was, that Susan—a gorgeous blonde who worked at ABC Escrow—had recently treated Larry to a delicious sushi luncheon, and Larry wished to repay her. Larry didn't think that countering the escrow company would be a deal-killer. After all, many listing agents request their choice of escrow and title services. So Larry wrote a counter offer that consisted of two sentences. It read: "Escrow company to be ABC Escrow instead of CBA Escrow. All other terms are acceptable."

Guess what happened? The buyer refused to sign this counter offer and when Larry called back to say, "My seller would accept CBA Escrow," the other agent told him, "Oh, gee, that's too bad. My client has just gotten his offer accepted on another property." Because of a simple counter offer, Mr. Alonzo's condo remained on the market for another six weeks!

BOB'S BOTTOMLINE *Any* counter offer written by a seller gives a buyer the chance to walk away from the sale. So in a slow market, be EXTRA careful about what you write.

If you don't wish to sweat over something little, don't be afraid to speak up.

Now, if you feel that ABC Escrow won't be objective, or if your settlement would be mishandled by Allan the incompetent attorney, than don't use those sources. But if the reason you wish to counter offer is because the fee is lower at the other company, why not play Columbo? In other words, before issuing a counter offer, call the escrow company or attorney's office and explain the situation. See if they will match their fee with your normal company. Nine times out of ten they will and you can avoid writing a counter offer!

CHANGE OF HEART

Steve and Melissa Annard were about to close escrow on the Sandlers' house. The Sandlers had already moved out of the house, and Steve and Melissa were being asked to vacate their apartment because the manager had already rented it to a new couple. Steve and Melissa had signed all their loan documents, and they had brought their money into escrow. Settlement was to take place on Monday.

Steve and Melissa called the Sandlers' realtor and asked if they could move into the house before the weekend. The realtor contacted the Sandlers. Trying to be accommodating, the sellers agreed to this arrangement, and Mark, their real estate agent drew up an interim occupancy agreement that included a "hold harmless clause."

The "hold harmless clause" was included to protect the seller in the event of theft of personal property as well as against liability in case someone became injured during the weekend. However, the same night that they moved into the property, Melissa Annard who drove a new Navigator and looked like a Playboy model, heard a strange humming noise when she took a shower.

The next morning, Melissa and Steve called Mark and put a halt to purchasing the home completely.

BOB'S BOTTOMLINE Sometimes buyers don't give any reason as to why they no longer wish to purchase, and until the deed records in a new buyer's name, any number of bad things can happen when the buyer is allowed to occupy a property prior to closing. A buyer can get mugged, injured or just get cold feet. A neighbor can be spying with a hidden camcorder, etc. etc. Therefore, allowing a purchaser to move into a property prior to closing escrow is somewhat like playing Russian roulette. You may have several successful outcomes but it takes only one time to discourage someone from continuing the practice. Before you rent back your home to any purchaser, get written legal advice on the letterhead of an attorney. Or simply tell the buyer, "My attorney has advised us against allowing the buyer to move into the house prior to closing."

STRICT REO RULES

Before we get into our next story, let me give you some background on corporate-owned or REO properties. REO is an acronym for "real estate owned" and generally corporate sales are handled by corporate asset managers who take their jobs seriously. There are urban legends about how some corporations sold houses for a hundred dollars, or how a corporate asset manager gave a property away to get it off the corporation's books. While there may be some great deals that have happened, generally corporate sellers treat property like any other seller. Why? Because people's jobs are at stake. A corporate asset manager could get fired for selling a house and not trying to get top dollar for the property. Therefore even when a bank or corporate seller has an unusually large amount of foreclosures on its books, you will still usually have to haggle back and forth on price. It's a business transaction and the corporate asset manager wants to prove to his superiors that he or she did a great job of getting top dollar for the company. In addition, buyers are advised to close escrow on time and as scheduled.

An agent named Bill once sold an REO property around the holidays to a buyer named James Michner. A tall, Bob Marley-like figure with dreadlocks, James worked in the entertainment business, and he had decided to take a month-long tropical vacation because the people in his industry would be on hiatus during the Christmas to New Year's holidays. When James finally returned from vacation, the escrow had gone four days over the originally projected closing date. James figured "no big deal," because the loan was already approved and James only had to sign his loan documents.

When James arrived at escrow ready to sign his papers, the escrow officer informed him, "I'm sorry James, but the REO company canceled escrow this morning."

"What?" thundered James. "My loan papers are here. I've got the money in the bank for the 30% down payment too." The escrow lady looked at him and shook her head. "The REO company instructed me to cancel everything because the escrow time period had been exceeded. Apparently they have found another buyer willing to pay more for the property."

BOB'S BOTTOMLINE Many buyers incorrectly assume that REO's, probates and government-owned properties do not require timely settlements. Not true. An REO asset manager will often receive offers from buyers while the property is in escrow, and will take the next buyer if escrow doesn't close on time. Therefore, if you happen to be going out of town the week of settlement, speak up and tell your agent. Also, whenever possible, ask for a few more days when initially submitting the REO contract. Example: a thirty-five day escrow instead of a thirty-day escrow. Do the same with a regular seller when the market is hot! If the seller feels that his property has increased in value, and the buyer hasn't closed escrow on time, the seller may speak up and use the closing date as a loophole to escape from selling the property.

CONTINGENCY BLUES

Pam and Gary Ingram were tired of their dreary little house so they listed with Barbie Broker, contingent upon the Ingrams finding and closing on a suitable property. Barbie posted the contingency remarks in the local MLS service, but Jerry, a broker from ABC Realty, never read the part about "subject to buying another home." So when Jerry brought a full-priced contract on the property, Pam and Gary's faces erupted into luminous smiles. They didn't notice that Jerry's contract made NO mention of the point that the sale was contingent on their finding another house. In

the presence of their agent Barbie, Pam and Gary signed the offer without making a counter offer regarding their contingency issue.

A few days later, the Ingrams found a suitable home and signed a contract on it, but the deal fell apart because of basement flooding problems discovered on the home inspection.

"I guess it wasn't meant to be," Gary told Pam. "I think we should stay here."

He called Barbie. "Could you please call Jerry and tell him that the deal is off?"

When Barbie called Jerry, he got angry. "Our transaction was never written subject to the seller finding another home," he exclaimed. "The seller entered into a legally binding contract to sell the house, and according to this agreement, the house would be vacant at closing. That's the way my buyer expects it to be."

BOB'S BOTTOMLINE

If you are selling your house subject to finding another home, speak up if you don't see the contingency phrase, "subject to and contingent upon seller's new purchase" included in every purchase contract as well as the listing agreement. In this case, things worked out okay because the buyer agreed to let the sellers "rent-back" their home for one month in order to find a suitable replacement property. But what if they couldn't find another suitable home? It might have been another sale from hell!

THE DASHED SELLERS

Tania and Mark were selling their home in Los Angeles by owner. Dean and Cindy visited the home on a Sunday when Tania happened to be baking fresh bread, and the young buyers fell in love with the house. The two couples wrote up an agreement on a form purchased at a stationery store.

However, the buyers made certain that the contract included a contingency clause. The purchase was contingent upon Cindy's grandfather's approval because her grandfather was going to be providing the down payment.

"My grandfather lives in Texas," Cindy explained. "He said he would give me the down payment money for my inheritance, so it shouldn't be a problem."

Ten days later, the buyers had a home inspection and all went well, so Tania and Mark made a non-contingent offer on a house in San Diego. After all, they felt that their house was sold! The seller of the San Diego house in turn made an offer on a house in San Clemente.

Three days before escrow was about to close, the row of dominoes collapsed. Cindy's grandfather, a sun-dried dirt-farmer from Texas, drove all the way to California to inspect the house, took one look at it and remarked, "No way. I'm not giving you that money to spend on this house." In tears, Cindy called Tania and Mark to tell them that the deal was off. That's when the fan hit the chandelier.

The dashed sellers received angry calls from people in San Clemente and San Diego. Everyone was pointing fingers at them and threatening long, expensive lawsuits.

BOB'S BOTTOMLINE Whenever you commit to buying another home, be prepared for the worst that can happen and hopeful for the best. In this case, the worst that could happen was that the buyer wouldn't be able to get the down payment from her relative. So as a seller, you need to speak up about getting this contingency removed within the first ten days of acceptance. Thus, a good counter offer might be, "This offer is subject to Grandpa's written disapproval within ten days of acceptance of the offer. In the event escrow does not receive written disapproval within ten days, it shall be deemed approved." In addition, the sellers should ask the buyer to put a large deposit (3% of the sales price) into escrow. That way, if the grandfather doesn't come through after the ten days, the buyer would stand to lose this deposit.

LAST MINUTE LENDER

Sharon and Eddie Balsam knew as much about buying a house as an old wooden fence. They brought all their income documentation to Sharon's high-school friend, Josie who was their loan broker. Josie made copies of all their paperwork and then said in a soothing tone, "Don't worry about a thing. Everything's going to be fine."

The Balsams found the perfect home where the sellers were pleasant. Everything went along smoothly until five days before the closing.

"Hello Sharon, this is Josie," said their loan broker. "The underwriter needs you to fax all of your paperwork to me again."

"All thirty pages?" Sharon asked.

"Yes, apparently a few pages are missing."

Sharon visited her real estate agent's office and had him re-fax all the documents to the loan broker's office. Two days before closing, Josie called again.

"Sharon, this is Josie, I forgot to tell you something. You keep faxing me pages one and two of your bank statements, but we also need pages three and four —even if those pages are blank. In addition, the underwriter needs your latest paystubs and an updated preliminary title report from escrow. If the underwriter doesn't get these documents by tomorrow, we won't get loan approval."

"I already gave notice on my apartment," Sharon fretted. "Plus my husband won't get his next paycheck till next Friday. Can't you use the last paystub?"

"No. His raise didn't show up on his last paystub."

"What if his boss writes a letter? Will that help?"

"We have a letter from his boss in our file, but the underwriter is requiring one paystub. It looks like we'll have to wait until next Friday until we can order loan documents."

In the meantime, the "nice" sellers were turning hostile because Josie was ducking their phone calls afraid to tell them what was happening. Another horror story was brewing as the scheduled closing date passed by and both buyers and sellers were anxiously wondering and worrying when and if this transaction would close.

BOB'S BOTTOMLINE

BOTTOMLINE Waiting for final loan approval can be about as much fun as sitting on death row, hoping for a last-minute reprieve from the governor! There's nothing worse than scrambling around at the last minute hoping to get loan approval—except that is, getting declined at the last minute. Now sometimes the last-minute lender documentation requests are reasonable. But then there are the times when the loan broker changes the loan program and neglects to tell anyone what they've done or why they've done it.

If there's a delay on your loan approval, find out the cause of the delay so that everyone can stay on the same course of action. Forget whose fault it was. The key is to close the transaction, because buyers aren't the only ones who worry. To a seller who sees the closing date pass and frets for the buyer's loan to be approved, it can seem like they were misled about the creditworthiness of the prospect from the start. So it's important for lenders, agents and all parties to keep the lines of communication open, and to return phone calls promptly or at least by the end of the business day. Besides, fretting causes wrinkles and who needs those, right?

Lesson Five Final Comments

Every profession has its share of charlatans and cheaters, and the real estate industry is no exception. Don't be afraid to speak your mind, but also be prepared to listen. Trying to read meaning into why a transaction is taking longer is pointless without knowing all the facts. Pop the bubble of silence or be prepared to read your own sorry tale in another edition of *Real Estate Sales from Hell!*

My bathroom has a digital sink. That's right, a digital sink. Every time I want the water to stop running, I put my finger in the faucet.

—Ron Smith

THINK
OUTSIDE THE BOX

THERE WAS ONCE A MAN who was looking to hire a person who could think quickly under pressure, so after setting up job interviews with fifty applicants, he asked each one of the job seekers how they would answer the following question. "You are driving your new car late one rainy night when you see three people standing under a lamppost. All three would like to get out of the rain, but you can only pick up one of them. The first person is your best friend who you've known all your life. The second person is an old lady having a heart attack. The third person is the love of your life. Who would you choose to pick up in your new car and why?"

Now I'll be honest, I jotted down that I would take the old lady having a heart attack. She seemed to be the person most in need, and I probably would have been happy to drive her to the nearest hospital in my new car. But my answer isn't the correct one. Here is the job-winning solution. "Since the first person is a friend that I could trust, I would give him or her the keys to my new car to take the old lady to the hospital. Then I would spend some romantic quality time huddling for warmth with the love of my life."

This kind of creative thinking is sometimes referred to as "thinking out of the box." In real estate, it's important to think creatively because you don't always get lucky. Sometimes you may have to bypass preconceived notions of how to get things done in order to successfully close a transaction and/or avoid a hellish experience.

OUT OF GAS

Manny Mercado was purchasing a large single-family home directly from Vincent Gilman. Because English was a second language to Manny, he asked Beatriz Rodriguez to draw up the paperwork for him, and act as his agent in the purchase for a flat fee.

Beatriz agreed to do this, and besides writing up the contract, she sent the seller a package of disclosures to fill out. Vincent, the seller, was fearful of putting anything in writing since the property had been a rental and he wasn't certain about its exact condition. Still, Beatriz was able to convince Manny to hire a home inspector. However, on the day of the inspection, the gas hadn't been turned on, so the home inspector couldn't tell if the stove, heater or hot water heater were functioning properly.

"What should I do?" Manny asked Beatriz.

"Let's ask the seller to turn the gas on, then have the items re-inspected by the home inspector."

Vincent, however, did not wish to incur the expense of turning on the gas, so Beatriz went to Manny's defense and thought outside the box. "If you don't turn on the gas, then the buyer demands that escrow withhold three thousand dollars from the seller's proceeds after closing until these items are tested," said Beatriz. "Because in a worse case scenario, Manny may need to replace the entire heating system, plus the stove and hot water heater. He won't be able to do so after settlement. That's why we need three thousand dollars to be withheld."

"In that case, I'll have the gas turned on," Vince griped.

The home inspector discovered that the stove and heater were in excellent condition but not the hot water heater. The seller agreed to replace it and the transaction closed successfully.

BOB'S BOTTOMLINE It helps to think out of the box prior to settlement! Because asking for a seller to fix an item after closing escrow is like trying to put toothpaste back into the tube. Technically, it may be feasible but it's difficult to accomplish. Also, if the seller cannot supply receipts of repair work and you are uncertain as to whether the seller has properly made the requested repairs, ask your home inspector to accompany you on the walk-through inspection prior to closing escrow.

LUCKY LUIS

One of the most frightening faxes I've ever received came from Hud (The U.S. Dept. of Housing and Urban Development). Normally, HUD conducts a sealed bid auction for residential real estate via the Internet. The real estate agent uploads the client's bid to the HUD Website. After all the bids are tabulated, the person with the highest net bid to HUD is considered the apparent winning bidder.

My clients, Luis and Maria Rodriguez, wrote an offer on a HUD home and we were named the apparent winning bidder. Hooray! However, Luis and Maria's loan broker failed to tell me that Luis and Maria needed a co-signor.

Not knowing this, I never wrote the co-signor's name on the purchase contract. The loan broker assumed that the co-signor's name could be added on later in escrow.

Two weeks later, I received a fax from HUD stating that HUD wished to rescind our winning contract.

"Why do they want to rescind?" I nervously asked the escrow officer.

"Your loan broker wishes to add somebody else to the contract."

"So, what's wrong with that?"

"It's HUD's policy that the names of ALL the purchasers must be on the original purchase contract approved by HUD. You can delete names with the consent of HUD, but not add them. Otherwise the contract is invalid."

"What's going to happen to the property?"

"Your buyers will get their earnest money deposit back and the house will go back on the market again."

That's the rule and that's exactly what happened.

Man, was I moody! I sulked like a preteen-adolescent after a scolding.

But once the house came back on the market, ALL of my buyers signed the purchase contract. Luckily, Luis won the bid again. Whew!

BOB'S
BOTTOMLINE Sometimes it pays to think "inside the box." Properties sold by HUD, the VA, and other government agencies, for example, have their own special forms, rules and guidelines—as do most REO companies, relocation companies and probate sales. If all the necessary forms aren't properly signed or are missing, you may lose a house to someone else!

LOCKED OUT!

Allan Poe looked like he had chronic fatigue and had lost too much weight recently. A thin, balding man with thick glasses, Allan was two months away from a foreclosure sale. Allan had already moved out of his townhome and luckily a buyer was about to close escrow on the property. However, when the purchaser visited the property one last time to conduct a final walk-through, something unexpected happened. Allan's agent, Jill Nash, tried to open the door for the buyer, but discovered that the key she fetched from the lockbox didn't work anymore. A note posted on the door from Allan's lender revealed that the bank had changed Allan's locks—even though Allan was still the legal owner!

"I'm not going to bring my money to close the transaction until I see the property one more time," said the buyer. She then drove away unhappily.

"I can't believe the bank did this! Can they legally do this?" Allan asked Jill almost in tears. "After all, I am still the owner of the house. What should I do?"

"Call the bank, and tell them that you need to get a key to do a final walk-through inspection," Jill advised. "Since you are still the owner, the bank cannot deny you the right to enter your own property."

Sure enough, after Allan made the call, the bank sent a key via overnight mail to Allan' new residence. The purchaser had her final walk-through inspection and escrow closed successfully.

BOB'S BOTTOMLINE Not all lenders change locks but those that do only re-key a property when they find that it's vacant. Now Allan could have called a locksmith to re-key the lock again, however be aware that the bank would then re-key the changed locks. So don't be afraid to simply call your bank while in foreclosure. Good communication with the bank will help towards a successful transaction.

WEEKEND PLANS

Michael and Sara Marx were purchasing their first home and needed to be out of their apartment by Friday. There was a three-day weekend and they had lined up all their friends to help them move over the holiday. Luckily, the house that they were buying was vacant, and the deed was supposed to record on Friday afternoon.

Unfortunately, when their real estate agent, Peter Abrahams, called escrow, the escrow officer told Peter:

"Sorry Peter, but there's been a snafu with the County Recorder's office. We still don't have confirmation from the title company that the deed has actually recorded yet. The title company may call us by six o'clock tonight, or we may not receive confirmation until Tuesday morning at nine o'clock. Remember Monday is a holiday!"

At six o'clock that evening, Peter called escrow to see if the deed had recorded in the names of the new buyers, but the office was closed for the long weekend.

Peter called the seller's agent and asked if Michael and Sara could move in the next morning, but the seller refused.

"This isn't fair," Michael complained. "We've done everything asked of us. Besides, the house is vacant, and since the loan funded, technically we're paying for it. In addition, we don't have any money for a hotel room. And our friends are lined up to help us move tomorrow. Can't you please have the sellers open the door for us?"

"It's not my house," Peter answered. "But let me call the sellers and see if they will allow me to give you the key."

Unfortunately, the sellers still refused to let Michael and Sara move into the home, and the young couple had to wait until Tuesday morning to get their keys, ruining their weekend plans. In the minds of Michael and Sara, they had just experienced a sale from Beelzebub's inferno that they'll never forget.

BOB'S BOTTOMLINE This situation comes up often in real estate, and the solution is surprisingly simple if you think outside the box. Don't schedule escrow to close on a Friday—especially if it's at the end of a month. Instead, make sure that settlement occurs any day from Monday through Thursday. That way, if there is a last-minute snafu, the weekend plans won't be ruined. For example, if Michael and Sara's settlement had originally been scheduled for Thursday, the sellers would have received confirmation on Friday morning, and the buyers could have still moved in over the long weekend!

FENCE FOLLIES

Bertha and Tim were excited about purchasing an REO property. The house needed carpet and paint, but it spanned over 2,000 square feet and it featured a large swimming pool which currently was dry. The corporate seller demanded that the house be sold in "as-is" condition and would not do any repairs. A week before closing, however, a problem developed.

The buyers' lender required that the seller install a fence around the empty pool as a safety precaution or they wouldn't fund the loan. However, the corporate seller was selling the house in "as-is" condition, and refused to do this.

"Bill, we told you that we are selling this property 'as-is,'" the listing agent reminded the selling agent. "You'll have to come up with all-cash or your buyers will lose their earnest money deposit."

The buyers were caught in a catch-22 situation that is typical with many "fixer-upper" properties. The bank sells the property at a reduced price because the house needs work. However, many times the purchase lender won't fund the buyer's loan until the work is done. And many buyers feel reluctant or afraid to do any work until the property actually belongs to them.

At a time like this, it takes someone to think outside the box to end the stalemate!

In this instance, Bill called the buyers lender and asked a dumb question. "How will the lender know if the fence has actually been installed by the seller?"

"They will send an inspector or appraiser out to the property to see that the fence is there."

"But won't that take a lot of time? I mean, this is a REO property and they are very strict about the closing date. Isn't there a faster way we can do this?"

"What are you suggesting?" the buyer's lender asked Bill.

"I've got a digital camera. Can't I take a photograph and email it to you?"

"Let me get back to you on that."

The buyer's lender called him back and agreed that an emailed photograph of the fence surrounding the dry pool would be sufficient for them to fund the loan. Mysteriously when Bill visited the property, a local "rent-a-fence" company had already set up a temporary fence around the pool! Imagine that! So Bill was able to snap a photograph of the fence surrounding the pool. After he emailed the photo to the lender, the loan funded and escrow closed successfully.

BOB'S BOTTOMLINE Calling a company to set a temporary fence around a pool without the property owner's consent is risky, however an argument can be made that the intent is to make certain that the corporate asset is safe—just as banks re-key properties so that people won't damage property that is sitting vacant. After all, if there are neighborhood children nearby, shouldn't a concerned citizen surround a dry pool with a fence?

GARAGE GRIPES

Elaine was a wiry, energetic woman who could eat like a Teamster but never gain an ounce. She lived with her cat in an apartment that was about to be demolished. Raven-haired Elaine purchased a house that was vacant and asked if she could move her boxes into the garage prior to the close of escrow. Elaine planned to stay with friends, but since she worked six days a week, she only had Sunday to move. The seller agreed to let her store her things in the garage on Sunday as long as Elaine promised NOT to move anything into the premises.

"I promise you I will not move anything beyond the garage," said Elaine. "Thank you so much."

Escrow prepared a document that was signed by both the seller and buyer allowing Elaine to have access to the garage but not the house. Julia, the listing agent gave Elaine a key to the garage side door to allow her access into the garage. "Once you're inside the garage, you can press the button for the automatic door opener which will open the big garage door," Julia explained.

That Sunday, Elaine used the key to the garage side door. Once inside the garage, she discovered an unlocked door that lead from the garage into the house. Elaine thought to herself, "Oh, the seller must have changed her mind. She's allowing me to have access into the house after all."

The following day, the seller decided to check on Elaine's move. The seller looked through a window, and lo and behold, she spied Elaine's refrigerator, sofa and various boxes inside the house.

"This is not acceptable," the seller fumed. "The buyer has broken the agreement and has stored items in the house without my permission!"

The seller was madder than a female pit bull with PMS. So she called escrow to cancel everything! After spending an entire morning on the phone with the listing agent Julia, the seller finally allowed escrow to close. After the closing, the seller filed a complaint against Julia for not properly supervising the buyer's move into the house.

BOB'S BOTTOMLINE This is a case of not thinking outside the box. Julia knew that her seller didn't wish to have the buyer gain access into the house and that her buyer needed access for the garage. Therefore Julia should have locked the door leading into the kitchen from the inside, and then given Elaine the remote key to the automatic garage opener. That way, the buyer would not have been able to enter the house but would have still had access to the garage!

SECTION 8 HEADACHE

Andy and Imelda Johnson wished to do something about their retirement. They were tired of receiving a low rate of return from having their money sit in the bank. They came to Bill's real estate office with the thought of purchasing some rental property.

"Have you ever considered purchasing a Section 8 property?" Bill asked.

"What is Section 8?"

"Section 8 was created for low-income housing. The way it works is the United States government guarantees a certain amount of rent per month, and the tenant pays the difference. In our area, for example, the average rent is $1,150. From this amount, the government guarantees $775, and the tenant usually pays about $375 per month. Because of the low interest rates available, with $10,000 down, if you were to purchase a home for $105,000, your payments would be about $811 including taxes and insurance. What this means to you is that you would make about $340 per month on your $10,000 investment."

So what made this tale a story from the devil and the deep blue sea?

Bill's purchasers made an offer on a property that had been accepted for Section 8 housing, where the U.S. government was paying $775 per month and the listing agent claimed the tenant was paying $375 per month. However, after the offer had been accepted, Bill learned that this tenant was actually paying $250 per month.

"It's your problem," said the listing agent. "You never wrote that the offer was contingent upon receiving a certain rental amount. Perhaps the tenant will move out prior to closing escrow and you can easily find a new tenant to rent this house." However, the tenant did not wish to move out unless Bill or the new buyers could find a suitable house for the same amount of rent. Or a similar replacement house near her mother. However, finding a house in Los Angeles that rents for $250 per month would be next to impossible!

BOB'S

BOTTOMLINE Thinking outside the box can also mean using the Internet to dig up fresh information. In this case, Bill could do a Google search for brokers and Section 8 housing for Las Vegas, Nevada and find a suitable replacement dwelling. Why Las Vegas? Because the tenant had mentioned that she wouldn't mind living near her mother who lives at the Oasis in the Desert—aka Las Vegas.

Lesson Six Final Comments

It's estimated that 97% of all millionaires made their money through real estate. The irony is that most of these millionaire investors purchased properties using *other* people's money. How did they do it? By thinking out of the box. Nowadays, for example, many lenders make zero-money down payment loans. How? The lender makes two loans. One is for the down payment. It will be 20% of the purchase price and will be secured against the property as a second trust deed. The new first loan will be for 80% and have no private mortgage insurance. Now you may not become a millionaire, but perhaps you can purchase a house this way too! To order a special report on How to Become Wealthy by Investing in Real Estate visit www.salesfromhell.com

What's the deal with people burning incense in their houses? Do they really think it's going to make their home smell better? It's like they set fire to the clothes hamper at the men's gym and all the gym socks, towels and jocks started burning.

—*Anonymous*

LESSON 7

THINGS AREN'T ALWAYS WHAT THEY SEEM

One night a fire started inside the local chemical plant. An alarm went out to all the fire departments from miles around, and after fighting the fire for an hour, the chemical company president announced: "Our secret formulas are in the vault in the center of that plant. They must be saved! I'll give $50,000 to the fire engine company that brings them out safely." Two hours passed by, and the president raised the amount to $100,000, then $300,000, and then a staggering one million dollars!

Suddenly, a siren was heard that came from a great distance away. It was a group of volunteer fire fighters composed entirely of men over sixty-five. To everyone's amazement, the little fire engine raced through the chemical plant, drove straight into the middle of the inferno, and saved the secret formula.

Overjoyed, the company president personally thanked each one of the volunteers, then he asked the group what they intended to do with the reward money. The fire truck driver looked him right in the eye and said, "The first thing we're going to do is fix the brakes on that truck."

I mention this story because the lesson in this chapter involves recognizing that sometimes in real estate, things aren't always what they seem to be.

MOTHER KNOWS BEST

Irma and Frank Thomas lived in a complex where the condominium units were huddled so close together that if they were any closer it would have been adultery. I mean you could almost hear the plants growing in the place next door. The Thomases listed their condo for only $165,000 and even agreed to carry the entire financing at an interest rate of 6% for 30 years with a 10% down payment. A buyer named John Smith gave them a $4,000 deposit which Irma put into escrow. Then, six days after acceptance, John's mother— who will be helping with childcare— decided that she didn't approve of the place.

"You're going to pay that much for that condo? What have you been smoking?" she remarked.

"But mom, you should see the other places we've looked at recently," replied John. "This is a great deal!"

"I don't care. I'm not going to help you baby-sit your kids if you buy that condo," John's mother pouted. "Find another place!"

Stressed out and emotionally spent, John canceled the transaction, and naturally Irma and Frank assumed that they would be allowed to keep his $4,000 deposit.

"After all, we agreed to everything in the contract," Irma pointed out. "Besides, there was no financing contingency. We agreed to finance their loan, and we had approved the buyers' credit. Therefore, since John Smith wishes to back out of the deal, we get to keep his earnest money deposit."

BOB'S BOTTOMLINE Unfortunately, in California, the Thomases won't get the money that easily. Most escrow companies will NOT release the buyer's deposit to the seller no matter how strong the seller's case is, unless the buyer also agrees to sign a release agreement. If the buyer refuses to sign it and the escrow deposit is less than $5,000, the seller's remedy is to take the buyer to small claim's court. If the deposit is more than$5,000, the seller may have to take the buyer to arbitration, mediation or court unless the two parties agree to a compromise.

HOOP HORRORS

Dania and Mario Green were a handsome young couple who purchased a condominium with a Homeowner's Association that required a mandatory fee of $150 per month. Mario liked to play basketball, and set up a hoop above his garage door. A week later, the Greens received a letter from the Homeowner's Association requesting them to remove their basketball hoop as it was against the regulations of the Association. The letter stated that if the hoop wasn't down by Friday the 13th, the Greens would be fined by the Association.

Mario removed the hoop on the 12th, but on his next statement from the Association, Mario discoverd a $50 fine.

Feeling that an injustice had occurred, Mario wanted to call attorney Johnny Cochran but couldn't afford his legal services, so instead he called his wife.

"I'm not going to pay this fine. I'll pay the regular amount, but there's no way in hell I'm going to pay this fifty-dollar fine. It's a matter of principle."

Dania sent in the regular payment, but the Association refused to honor her check. Every month for three months, Dania sent her normal payment, but the Association returned it without cashing the check. Dania assumed that eventually things would get straightened out.

The next letter the Greens received was from the Association's lawyer, notifying them that a lien of $1,250 had been filed against the Greens' property for non-payment of their Association fees. The Greens were facing the possibility of losing their house to foreclosure over a lousy $50 fine!

BOB'S BOTTOMLINE Life is often not fair, and the sad truth is that some Homeowner's Associations and their presidents uniformly fine association members with the glee and enthusiasm of a Marine drill sergeant. Therefore, it's wiser to pay the $50 fine first, and then to protest it. Hopefully the Greens would win their case in small claim's court. But because $1,000 of the $1,250 goes to pay the Association's attorney, even in a worse case, if the Greens don't prevail, they would only be out the $50 fine and not any late fees, attorney's fees or any other miscellaneous foreclosure fees.

HOUSE ON RAT HILL

Mary Thompson was as pretty as a well-dressed iguana. But to Mary's realtor, Jeff Landeu, her money looked as gorgeous as any fashion model's. Jeff convinced Mary to purchase a brownstone built in the middle of fashionable Beverly Hills for $4,500,000. Because of the price of the house, Mary assumed that it was in excellent condition. "The prior owners were movie stars with tons of money," gushed Jeff. One month after moving in, Mary heard the sound of tiny footsteps in the attic, and when she climbed the ladder into the attic, she made a sudden and horrifying discovery.

"Rats! There must be hundreds of them! This place is infested!"

Mary laid some traps, but the next morning, she discovered evidence that her bathroom has been invaded by her rat "roommates" during the night.

"What's going on? Is this a new plague or did that scoundrel sell me a house on a rat hill?"

BOB'S BOTTOMLINE

Things aren't always what they seem. Even a gorgeous house in Beverly Hills can be infested with rats, mice, ants, cockroaches, spiders, moths, termites or even bats! Across the country, so many homeowners have encountered infestation-from-hell stories that they are now almost a cliché. However, in most states across the U.S., lenders require a pest inspection report clearance prior to funding a loan, so the first step would be to check with the person who did the pest control report. Usually that company will come out and treat a problem for free if it has occurred within the first twelve months after you've purchased the home. If they won't, check your home warranty policy. Many policies now include pest problems as well as home defects. If you live in an area that doesn't require a clean bill of health from a pest control inspection report prior to settlement, you are advised to obtain one.

A HUMAN RAT

Kent Meadow was a man determined to sell his house "by owner" because he had sold several houses of his own in the past. A shrewd horse-trader, Mr. Meadow was one of those folks who believe that people will have no respect for you unless you frighten them a little, and he acted like he held a grudge against all mankind. He wore a chip on his shoulder proudly, almost defiantly, and showed it to any real estate person who tried to get him to list.

Mr. Meadow wished to sell his house for $203,000, which was a little high. Still, one day a buyer named Mark King made Mr. Meadow an offer for $202,500. The deal called for Mark to get a bank loan for $150,000 as long as Mr. Meadow would agree to carry a second trust deed for the balance. The way Mark wrote his offer, the second trust deed would be subordinate to any new first deed. "This way," Mark explained, "it will be easier for me to obtain a new first loan and then I'll make payments directly to you on the second loan of $52,500 which I expect to pay off in three years."

Mr. Meadow agreed to this proposal, escrow was opened at Shady escrow, and settlement closed on time as scheduled.

Three months later, Mr. Meadow was angrier than a teenager who'd been grounded. He wanted to get his hands on Mark because this buyer had made only two payments and then stopped. And so Mr. Meadow went back to his old house to pay Mark a visit.

To his horror, Mr. Meadow discovered that Mark had never even moved into the property. Making matters worse, Mark had taken out a new first loan in the amount of $875,000, and he hadn't made a single payment on that loan. Apparently, Mark had found a crooked appraiser who was willing to appraise the property for $1,200,000. It seems that this appraiser had used comparable sales of million-dollar houses located at the top of Mr. King's street. Because the agreement stated that the second would be subordinate to *any new first trust deed* that Mark could obtain, the escrow company had sent an amendment to Mr. Meadow regarding the first trust deed of $875,000 along with a slew of other papers. Mr. Meadow had signed all the papers without carefully reading them.

Eventually the bank foreclosed on the loan for $875,000 for lack of payment. This extinguished Mr. Meadow's equity of $52,500. Eventually, the police did catch up with Mark King, his loan broker and the crooked appraiser. They threw these individuals in prison, but this transaction left Mr. King poorer by $52,500 and with an even nastier taste in his mouth!

BOB'S BOTTOMLINE

This horror story actually happened to some folks in Encino, California during the early 1980's. It's fine to sell a home "by owner," but before signing anything, have any and all contracts and addendums reviewed by a competent real estate attorney. Nowadays, in California, any loss by a lender for a negligent or fraudulent appraisal would be shifted to the loan broker.

FAULTY INSPECTION

Karen Yang had beautiful eyes and a silent, Buddah-like detachment to making decisions. In this situation, she wished to obtain a home inspection prior to purchasing her home.

"I'm unfamiliar with home inspection services," Karen told her real estate agent Mary Smith. "Which company would you use if you were me?

"Everyone in my office uses Wally so I assume that he's the best," Mary blabbed. "Here's his phone number. Call him up. He's been around forever."

Wally certainly did seem to know what he was doing, and Karen enjoyed his breezy manner as he walked through the house and filled out a preprinted form.

Twelve days after escrow closed, however, Karen noticed several items missing on Wally's preprinted report, as well as things that were clearly inaccurate. Among the problems missing that Wally didn't detect was a chimney damper that wouldn't close, for example. Also, a large crack ran from one side of the chimney to the other. Because of this large crack, Kim was afraid of using the fireplace.

Kim called Mary on the telephone. "I just wanted you to know that I have a big problem with my chimney," she told Mary. "So in the future it might be wise not to refer Wally. He did a terrible job. Not only that, when I checked with the state licensing board, they told me that his license had been revoked last year."

BOB'S BOTTOMLINE Things aren't always what they appear to be. Most real estate companies routinely hand pamphlets of home inspection companies to a buyer and assume that they are reputable. Do not assume that any references of these referrals have been recently checked. Therefore, even if a real estate person highly recommends a home inspector, or gives you a list of three home inspectors, be prepared to play Colombo. Call around to make certain that the inspector is experienced in construction defects (some are not) and has insurance for any errors or omissions he or she might make.

NOT FUNDED

Gloria and Thomas Murphy owned seven properties. When listing a rental property, their trusted real estate advisor Carl suggested that they draw up a trust in case something happened to either one of them. Mrs. Murphy called Terry Givens, an attorney who specialized in trusts and Terry set up a revocable living trust for the Murphys. Three years after signing their trust, Thomas died of a heart attack, and Gloria wished to sell the house because of all the memories.

However, when Gloria called Carl to list the house, he had some bad news for her. "Gloria, your trust was never funded."

"What do you mean?" she asked.

"Your properties were never put into the trust. To make

the trust legal, you and Thomas needed to transfer each property into the trust."

"Didn't we do that? I assumed that we did that when we signed everything."

"No. To do so, you would need to sign separate quitclaim deeds or grant deeds on each of the seven properties, deeding them to the trust, so the ownership of each property would read 'Gloria and Thomas Murphy, trustees of the revocable living trust.'"

BOB'S BOTTOMLINE A living trust is just a sheaf of papers unless it is funded. Don't spend your time and hard-earned money on a trust if you don't intend to transfer your assets. Also, don't use a trust unless it clearly fits your financial and personal situation. Consult with an attorney or tax advisor about what might work best for you.

TRUTH IN ADVERTISING

I once took a buyer to see a house that was a real dump. I'm not boasting here, but this house was vying for the title of King of Squalor. The funny thing was that the buyer had the impression that it would be some kind of unique, charming little cottage. When I unlocked the front door, he reacted angrily with me. It was like he thought I was trying to steer him away from the real house. He demanded to see the house advertised under the heading "Investor's Special" that had sounded absolutely fantastic.

"What is so *special* about this dilapidated doghouse?" the buyer asked me. I tried to explain that the word "special" didn't mean "extraordinary," but more like "singular," "unique" or "out of the ordinary."

"It's called an 'investor's special,'" I explained, "because nobody else would dare purchase it but an investor with lots of money."

"Right," he said sarcastically. Then he showed me a classified ad that read "Walk to Everything." "What about this home?" the buyer asked.

"That one is located between Smokey's Nightclub and a gas station."

"How about this one? It's called 'Hidden Treasure.'"

"Umm. That house is located about fifty miles away from town. We'll never find it today unless we have a global positioning satellite to help us."

"How about 'Classic Character?'"

"Do you happen to have an extra hundred thousand dollars to spare?" I asked.

BOB'S BOTTOMLINE Classified advertisements for real estate are not always what they seem to be, and don't always match reality. Especially when inventory is short. That's when many agents stretch the truth and/or advertise the same listing under two or three different agents' names. Imagine the confusion that buyers feel as to why they see the same photograph of a home listed for the same price under three different headings and three different real estate agents! Overall, I believe care should be taken so that advertisements do match reality.

Lesson Seven Final Comments

In real estate, it's usually not a good idea to "assume" things because many times things aren't always what they seem. The credibility, professionalism and honesty of the real estate industry shouldn't be taken lightly so real estate agents should strive to match advertisements with reality. Worse is when a buyer finds out something derogatory after the closing that agents assumed they already knew. That's when long, expensive lawsuits become the order of the day.

EXPECT MIXED EMOTIONS

According to the 2002 edition of the Guinness Book of World Records, Thimble Hall, located in the village of Youlgreave, England holds the record for being the smallest detached house in the world. It measures 11 ft. 10 in. by 10 ft. 2 in. (3.63 m by 3.14 m) which is smaller than some closets. Incredibly, it was reputedly occupied by a family of eight in the 19th century! Ironically, the house with the most rooms is called Knole House, not far away in the village of Sevenoaks, England. This fortress-like building has 365 rooms, one for each day of the year.

Now I believe that the people who lived in both houses probably felt a tinge of mixed feelings when they moved out. On the one hand, the people might have experienced a feeling of relief at finally leaving such a small or big house. But on the other hand, there might have been folks who felt sad, nostalgic, or even a sense of loss for the time spent at that particular dwelling.

I may be stating the obvious. But nowadays many people are too tired, too stressed, or too involved in their careers to take this matter into consideration prior to moving. Not properly acknowledging the impact that a move has upon a person, I think is a mistake. Because often there's more to selling a house than just putting a sign in the yard and an ad in the paper. Problems can arise when people have mixed feelings.

MOUSE IN HOUSE

John and Virginia Jenkins were having the toughest time selling their house. It had been on the market for five months and they hadn't received even one offer. One day, Mrs. Jenkins overheard her eight-year-old son, Robbie, talking to his best friend, Joel.

"It's too bad that you have to move," said Joel.

"Oh I don't think we'll ever move to Georgia," Robbie told his buddy.

"Really? Why not?"

"My mom and dad don't know this, but about two months ago, I found a bunch of old mouse traps in the garage. I set them out by all the bedroom windows in the house. Then, on the back of all the informational brochures, I wrote: 'Beware: house infested with mice!'"

BOB'S BOTTOMLINE Many children feel nervous about moving to a new house, leaving old friends and meeting new people. Even some young-people who were easygoing and extroverted can suddenly become self-conscious, tongue-tied, and rebellious about attending a new school. Instead of assuming that a child who says nothing about moving is as happy and excited as you are, encourage the child to openly discuss his or her feelings with you about the move and then actively listen. Perhaps you might confront the child's fear of meeting new people by suggesting that the more you smile and are outgoing with people, the more you're going to get that back. As the Bible says, "you reap what you sow." Get involved, discuss the move and listen to your child, and if need be, solicit the help of a professional counselor.

GET RID OF THEM!

Mr. Mosely was a tall, slender, African-American man who felt very proud of his heritage and ancestors. And rightly so. A number of his friends and relatives have worked in high places in the American government and Mr. Mosely had collected many interesting photographs and articles about these folks and their accomplishments. These items had been framed and mounted on the walls of his home. In addition, he had memorabilia from his celebrity friends on the walls too. As a result, these famous faces, articles and more adorned almost every square inch of his wall space. The place reminded me of a museum.

In fact, at one open house, I must have spent half an hour just admiring all the old photographs. During that same open house, I realized that I wasn't the only one entranced by all the stuff on the walls. Everyone who walked through the front door seemed mesmerized by it.

"Wow, mom, look at this! A picture of Arthur Ashe, the tennis player. Here's one of Artis Gilmore, the pro basketball player. Oh, check this out. Here's Frank Sinatra, and look, a letter from Robert Kennedy!"

The hellish part for me was that Mr. Mosely happened to be the nicest guy you could ever meet, and yet I couldn't get his house sold. Then it dawned on me why people weren't buying. Although the personal belongings were charming, the house had the sex-appeal of a museum. But how could I convey this to Mr. Mosely?

After another unsuccessful open house, I asked Mr. Mosely, "Which is more important, Mr. Mosely, having everybody see your photographs and memorabilia, or selling your home?"

Mr. Mosely's face showed his mixed emotions. "Why, selling my home, I guess."

"If that's the case, I suggest that you remove 50% of the items from your walls and pack them up. Right now, people are more interested in checking out what's on the walls than in looking at your house."

Mr. Mosely's face tightened with anxiety, but then he radiated a serene dignity. "All right," he said. "Come back on Wednesday and tell me what you think."

The following Wednesday, I got a big surprise. Instead of packing up 50% of his photographs and memorabilia, why I'd say that Mr. Mosely had gotten rid of 90%. In addition, his nephew and his nephew's wife had painted the walls a light gold color and the place looked and smelled like a newer home.

For a fleeting second, I thought he might have gone too far. The walls seemed barren with everything packed up, but guess what happened? Mr. Mosely's house sold and he was so pleased that he gave me an autographed picture of his godfather. (Actually, it was a glossy photo of the singer, James Brown.) Granted, it could have been a coincidence that the house sold without the clutter. More likely, the house just seemed more spacious to a buyer.

BOB'S BOTTOMLINE Be sure that you're serious about selling. In fact, if you are in the process of selling your home, why not spend a minute and write down as a goal: "By June 15th our house will be sold." Now that your goal is in writing, pre-pack some of your personal belongings and then store the boxes in the garage. At first, the rooms may seem uncomfortably barren, but psychologically it gives you a head start and it aids a buyer in mentally moving their belongings into your space. Plus, by seeing all the boxes in the garage, a buyer may get the signal that you are serious about moving.

MIXED SIGNALS

Kathy and Lou Frazzle thought that their house was sold. Their buyers were satisfied with the home inspection. The termite report was completed, the appraisal went as planned, and the buyers received loan approval. The sellers even paid for the septic tank to be inspected and certified by a pumping company. However, their agent Susan Scott had waited until the last minute to give the buyers a transfer disclosure statement.

The transfer disclosure statement tells a purchaser about any actual or possible problems that the seller knows about the property.

After reading the seller's transfer disclosure statement, the buyers decided that they did not wish to purchase the Frazzles' home. The buyers claimed that it was because the disclosure indicated the house was located in a flood hazard zone and Mrs. Buyer was concerned that the place could possibly get flooded in the winter. She asked Lou Frazzle if the basement had ever flooded, and Lou answered, "Yes, but that's common around here." Susan Scott had assumed that the signing of the transfer disclosure was not a big deal. However, the buyers used the flood disclosure excuse to back out of the transaction.

A week later, over a cup of coffee, Lou heard that the buyers had purchased another home, two streets away, that was selling for $10,000 less than the Frazzle house.

BOB'S BOTTOMLINE

Some buyers will have mixed feelings after deciding to purchase a home, this is also known as "buyer's remorse." Because of this phenomenon, it's a good reason to disclose all actual and possible problems at the outset in writing during early inspections. Waiting for the last minute to have a buyer sign a disclosure about a flood hazard zone is not a good idea. It can make it seem like you were trying to hide something. If you never disclose the flood zone and the buyer finds out after closing, you might be in for a lawsuit. Addressing these kinds of environmental issues at the initial time of purchase allows the buyers more time to research and properly investigate the potential problem. Once the matter has been properly investigated, a buyer may lose their feeling of remorse.

NEW HOUSE HORROR

Dirk Schwartz and Janet Zimmer closed escrow on their old house and then the seller of the house they just bought allowed them to move their possessions into the new place before closing. Dirk and Janet felt incredibly happy because they had never lived in a brand new house. Two days after moving their things in, Dirk and Janet returned to their new home to discover that they'd been robbed! All of Dirk and Janet's household goods had been stolen!

Fortunately for this couple, Dirk had forgotten to cancel their insurance policy on their old house—the one they'd just sold. Since their new homeowner's insurance had not yet gone into effect because escrow hadn't yet closed, the homeowner's policy on their old house still covered their losses.

BOB'S BOTTOMLINE Mixed feelings sometimes show up when people drop the ball and forget to do something. Subconsciously, they may be resisting the move. In this case, it was not really a mistake but you can probably see how it could have become a nightmare. Before canceling an old insurance policy, make certain that a new policy is in place. Life moves on, so welcome the change.

THE NAKED LADY

James and Cindy Chang were anxious to buy a home. They worked long hours and had to meet me at 7 p.m. every night for a week to see homes. One evening, Mr. and Mrs. Chang and their son followed me as I walked up the sidewalk towards the front door to the first house. "I apologize for just showing up on your doorstep like a bunch of trick-or-treaters, but your telephone line was busy. Are you sure it's okay for us to see your home?" I asked the seller after he greeted us at the door. "It's no problem, come right in," the seller replied.

The four of us entered the seller's house. "Before we begin," I announced, "my buyers want to know if you have three bathrooms."

"Yes we do," said the seller. "There are two bathrooms upstairs and one downstairs. I'll show them to you." Mr. Seller practically sprinted down the hallway, so we all walked quickly along behind him. Then he flung open a door with a grand flourish. "Here is the downstairs bathroom."

I noticed all three of the Changs mouths sag open, so I had to look too. In my dirty little mind, I imagined that the seller's wife was nude or walking out of the shower wearing her freshly washed birthday suit.

Instead, she was like Lady Godiva with long blonde hair calmly sitting on the potty. She looked up from reading the newspaper and yelled, "Shut the door, please!"

BOB'S BOTTOMLINE Sometimes one person may be more excited about moving than the other family members. So try to discuss things with your loved ones, like the move in general and upcoming appointments with potential buyers. Knock before entering closed doors and respect other people's privacy or the mixed feelings of the mood can erupt into something ugly.

SELLING BY THE BOOK

I met Sam and Agnes Marston because they had posted a "For Sale By Owner" sign in front of their house. The Marston's allowed me to present my marketing ideas to them, but they insisted that they still wished to sell their home themselves.

Because the Marston's had never sold a house before, I gave them some advice. "If you are truly serious about selling by owner, buy one of those Nolo Press books at the local Barnes & Noble bookstore," I suggested. "Or buy one from their Web site: www.nolo.com . But don't try to sell by owner without some kind of guidance."

The Marstons took my advice and purchased a book. About a week later, I stopped by with a lead- base paint addendum. This addendum is required to be signed by most landlords and sellers in the United States, but many people, like the Marstons who sell "by owner" are not aware of it.

"Are you ready to list with me?" I asked.

"Not yet," said Mr. Marston.

One month later the Marstons came into my office. "Are you ready to list with me now?" I asked happily.

"Oh no, we sold our house," Mr. Marston announced.

"You did?" I remarked a little incredulously. After all, like most real estate agents, I usually have a superiority complex about this issue. Like nobody else in the world should be able to sell a house except a professionally trained realtor, right?

"Yes, our escrow is closing two weeks from Friday," said Mr. Marston.

"So, did you just drop by to rub it in?" I joked, smiling.

"That too, but actually, our plans have changed. We're thinking of staying here locally and we were wondering if perhaps you could help us find another house. That is, if you're interested."

"Of course, I'm interested. I'm just a little surprised since I was always stopping by your house to bug you about things."

"Actually, a few other agents did stop by the house too. But you were the only real estate agent who didn't make us feel bad for trying to sell it ourselves."

So that's how it happened. The Marstons purchased another home through me, and over a period of five years, they referred two of their friends to their real estate agent, Bob Boog.

BOB'S

BOTTOMLINE Some agents become nervous when they see books that try to help sellers sell their homes themselves, but many of these "by owner sellers" get mixed feelings about moving out of town and do end up purchasing locally. I do recommend that people list with a realtor to obtain the best exposure. However, if you're determined to sell direct, purchase a Nolo Press book and/or the "Guides for Dummies" publications. I think they provide valuable sources of information to the public. Selling a home is often not as easy as you might think because of the many details involved, but these books will help out with some situations.

COURT CONFIRMATION

Brandon and Sophie Weston had no illusions about themselves. They couldn't afford a big house. In fact, they could barely afford a little house so they were interested in purchasing a probate or a pre-foreclosure home. They drove around and searched for homes with yards that featured dead grass, weeds and old newspapers sunning themselves on the driveway or front porch.

Brandon found one such house and chatted with a neighbor who happened to know the owner's name and telephone number. The owner's name was Mr. Bryant and Brandon called him on the telephone several nights later.

"Hi Mr. Bryant, my name is Brandon Weston and I noticed that you own a house over on Spruce Street. I was wondering if you had ever thought about selling it."

"It's possible," said Mr. Bryant. "Why? Are you looking to buy?"

"Yes sir," Brandon told him.

"The house was owned by my mother and it's going through probate. There will be a sign on it next Saturday with the real estate company's phone number. The asking price is $200,000. You'll need to have a check for ten percent of the purchase price as an earnest money deposit if you're interested."

The following Saturday, Brandon and his wife found that they were the only ones at the realtor's open house. They liked the house so much that Brandon wrote an offer for

$201,000. The listing agent told Brandon, "Congratulations. There will be a court confirmation hearing one month from today. It isn't mandatory Brandon, but I suggest that you attend. I'll put a sold sign out and show this property as being sold in the computer." The listing agent gave Brandon the address for the court confirmation hearing and Brandon handed the agent the required 10% deposit.

Brandon's wife reminded him to attend the court hearing, but Brandon had cooled off to the house a little because of his rising mixed feelings. After all, he thought, we have to buy the house in "as-is" condition. What will happen if something doesn't work properly? He decided not to attend the confirmation hearing. After all, nobody showed up at the open house, did they?

Unfortunately, another purchaser did show up at the court confirmation hearing. He submitted a slightly higher bid than Brandon's. To his dismay, Brandon received his deposit check back in the mail. Brandon and his wife were back to square one.

BOB'S

BOTTOMLINE For most probates, it's important to attend the court confirmation hearing. Many purchasers avoid probate auctions and the court confirmations for fear that they will need to bring in all cash in order to purchase the property. Not true—at least not in Los Angeles County. The buyer only needs to have a 10% deposit in the form of a cashier's check. After the judge confirms the sale, an escrow will be opened and the balance of the purchase price may be financed. Simply bring a pre-approval letter to the court confirmation hearing and give it to the probate referee.

Sometimes a mini-auction will erupt in court and the property will be sold to the highest bidder. In the event of an overbid*, the balance of the 10% deposit can be made in the form of a personal check—so don't forget to bring your checkbook to the court confirmation hearing.

*Example: Sales price is $200,000, a purchaser would need a cashier's check for $20,000 to bid on the property. However, let's say that at the court confirmation, a mini-auction erupts, and the winning bidder offers $212,000. This would be an "overbid" offer.

Ten percent of $212,000 is $21,200. Subtract the original amount of $20,000 from $21,200 and you get $1,200. So in addition to the $20,000 cashier's check, the winning purchaser would give the estate a personal check for $1,200.

EXTENSION BLUES

Let's start off with some background. Properties sold by HUD, as well as many bank-owned properties and probates, have a "per diem" or daily rate written into their contracts. What this means to you is that the contract states that for each day that escrow goes past the scheduled escrow date, the buyer is charged $25 or $50 per day—whatever the "per diem" is that was stated in the fine print. The sum adds up quickly too.

I once sold a probate to Tommy, a handsome young buyer whose credit score was 655. Tommy's credit score showed that he had good credit and most lenders would give him a preferred interest rate. (In real estate lending, the best score is an 800 and the lowest score is a 400. Most conventional real estate lenders require a credit score of 620 or above in order to buy a home.)

Because the probate court had a sixty-day escrow, the lender ran a last-minute credit report. Tommy's credit score had dropped to 585 because he had forgotten to pay a credit card—his one and only credit card—on time. Tommy could still buy the home, but now he practically had to beg to obtain a "sub-prime" loan. This meant he would receive a higher interest rate. Instead of a $650 monthly payment, it would now be $950 dollars per month—all because of that one late credit card payment!

Tommy had mixed feelings about what to do. The first lender had already submitted loan documents to escrow, but the second lender had told him: "I'm confident that I can get your credit score back up to 650 in the next thirty days. That way, you'll get a better interest rate."

"What should I do?" Tommy asked me. "I hate to pay this crappy interest rate but escrow is supposed to close in three days. I'd like to wait to see if this new lender can really change my credit score."

"Take the crappy interest rate, close escrow and refinance later, " I advised him. "After all, what is the guarantee that your lender can successfully change your credit score in thirty days? What if it only changes upwards by ten points? There is a fifty dollar per day charge, and if you don't close escrow, you can lose your entire deposit. Therefore it's possible that you could pay an extra $1,500 in fines for being thirty days late, your credit score may not change one bit, plus you may be forced to forfeit your deposit."

The buyer signed his loan documents with the lousy interest rate and escrow successfully closed. Not long after, he refinanced too!

BOB'S BOTTOMLINE Some per diems like the ones from HUD must be paid in the form of a cashier's check in advance before escrow can proceed. If the buyer refuses to pay the per diem in advance, the buyer forfeits the earnest money deposit. In Los Angeles County, the earnest money deposit for a probate is 10% of the sales price, paid in the form of a cashier's check made out to the estate. Losing a deposit of 10% of a $200,000 sales price can represent a significant amount of money!

Lesson Eight Final Comments

Whether you buy or sell a home, expect to have mixed feelings about the situation. The important thing is to know that other people have survived similar circumstances as you. So, if possible, talk with friends, relatives and acquaintances who have been through the buying or selling process.

"A hooker came up and told me she'd do anything kinky for a hundred dollars. I told her to paint my house!"

—***Henny Youngman***

LESSON 9

PUTTING IT ALL TOGETHER

IN THE MOVIE *DIE HARD,* Bruce Willis gazes out a window from a high-rise building and watches a police car down below traveling in reverse. The car zigzags wildly at a high rate of speed and then it finally crashes. After watching the backwards moving car, Bruce shakes his head and comments, "Who was driving that car—Stevie Wonder?"

Likewise, some of the wild and wacky stories in this book may have you shaking your head because most people hope to have a good experience when selling their homes. To avoid a hellish type of situation from happening to you, learn from some of the lessons in this book. Beware of playing dumb, investigate situations like Detective Columbo would, and get things in writing. Also, remember that the real estate laws in your area may be totally different than mine, so follow the local laws. Hopefully, your experiences will not be as horrible as the ones found in these pages.

What I've found is that half of not having a sale-from-hell experience is simply being aware that these kinds of transactions have happened. Since you know that a small mistake can turn into something bigger down the line, why not use a simple tool that most successful real estate people utilize? It's called a "checklist." Most escrow and title companies preprint these checklists onto folders so that real estate agents can keep a better eye on their transactions. (See the list on the next page.) I've formatted a checklist into a series of questions that a buyer or seller can ask an agent. Getting the answers to the questions on this checklist may help you avoid a sale from hell and assist you in keeping a closer eye on a transaction.

WHAT ABOUT USING THE INTERNET?

Another tool to enable buyers, sellers and realtors to better facilitate transactions is a "transaction management platform" available on the Internet. A transaction management platform on a website allows buyers, sellers and their agents to check on the status of an escrow twenty-four hours a day without bothering anyone. Companies like www.dealtrack.com, www.bridgespan.com and www.gurunet.net offer such services. These management platforms can help organize the details and keep people informed about the progress of any transaction. For example, a buyer from Chicago can log onto the site to find out the status of an escrow in Arizona, or an agent in California and a seller in Paris could have a conference meeting on the platform to discuss a legal issue with an attorney in New York.

While the road of real estate is often bumpy, using an Internet transaction coordinator, or even the simple checklist mentioned earlier, may prevent you from becoming car-sick along the way.

CHECKLIST OF REAL ESTATE QUESTIONS

WEEK ONE

What is the Sales Price? ____________________ $355,000
Escrow number? ____________________ 2435-21MN
Escrow officer? ____________________ Margie Parks
Escrow's phone number? ____________________ (661) 555-5131
When was escrow opened? ____________________ 1-3-2003
Scheduled close? __ Approx. close of escrow: 1-30-2003 Thurs.
Deposit? ____________________ $8,000
Deposit brought to escrow? ____________________ 1-4-2003
Lender? __________ Wells Fargo/George Huan (661) 555-2121
Lender commitment letter received? ____________________ 1-5-2003

WEEK TWO

Home inspection? ____________________ 1-7-2003
Start time: ____________________ 2:30 p.m. Utilities on? Yes
Property disclosures signed? __ Seller: 1-7-2003, Buyer: 1-9-03
Escrow instructions signed? ____________________ 1-7-2003
CC&R'S and homeowner rules? ____________________ None
Home inspection response: ____________________ 1-12-2003
Did buyer/seller accept response? ____________________ Yes/No
Appraisal ordered? ____________________ 1-8-2003
Date of the appraisal inspection? ____________________ 1-13-2003
Termite ordered? ____________________ 1-8-2003
Date of the termite inspection? ____________________ 1-12-2003
Septic/well cert ordered? ____________________ 1-8-2003
Date of septic/well inspection: ____________________ 1-14-2003
Fire insurance ordered? ____________________ 1-14-2003

WEEK THREE

Loan documents in escrow? ____________________ 1-23-2003
Final walk-through inspection: ____________________ 1-25-2003

WEEK FOUR

Seller must give up possession by: __________ Sat. Feb 1, 2003
____________________ Approx time: 5:p.m.

MISC.

Keys to be delivered: _____ 2 garage remotes and 3 house keys
Where to pick up keys? ____________ Listing office will deliver.

IN THE REAL WORLD, UNEXPECTED STUFF OFTEN HAPPENS

Unfortunately, the truth is that not all real estate problems can be avoided by just using a checklist or the Internet. Recently, for example, I had a buyer who encountered a last-minute snafu that delayed the closing of escrow by a week. What happened? The seller had called his insurance company *three* years before because a branch had fallen and had done some damage. However, the seller decided to fix the damage himself. But because he had called the insurance company, they had created a claim. Technically, no insurance company could issue a new homeowner's policy for the buyer until the computer database showed that the old claim by the seller had been settled. Another client had a problem getting homeowner's insurance because the insurance agent had stopped inside the house to use the bathroom and noticed mold on the bathroom ceiling. In this case, we faxed a toxic mold disclosure that had been signed by the buyers, and an insurance company issued a new homeowner's policy. However, with more and more cases of toxic mold in California, who knows when a mold issue may become an even bigger problem down the line? In the future, buyers in California may be required to purchase mold insurance — the same way that buyers in some regions are required to obtain flood insurance.

YIN AND YANG

All things are continuously changing, and in real estate, this is especially true. Asian literature refers to this constant change as Yin and Yang. According to this belief, everything in the universe is a matter of balance. Change swings back and forth like a pendulum. Savings yields to spending. Inflow leads to outflow. The passive power changes to active. So if your real estate market has been charging forward, according to Yin and Yang, get ready for it to balance backward.

In addition, consider the following. Most people, when they think about constant change and leading a balanced life, are concerned about stress and/or not eating properly. Eating the right food and relaxing to achieve balance — these factors are important. But because life is mostly activity, factors that are also important in achieving balance are what we do overall and how we think on a daily basis. In particular, the part our actions and daily thinking play in a real estate transaction can very much affect its outcome. So chew on the following food for thought when dealing with any real estate transaction as well as everyday life.

FOOD FOR THOUGHT

Benjamin Franklin attributed the key to his own success to this quote: "I will speak ill of no man and all the good I can of everyone I meet."

I've noticed that successful people take one more step forward. They not only *speak* all the good of everyone they meet, they also *think* all the good of everyone they meet. They have a tremendous "giving" attitude. In addition:

1. They are able to laugh when they make a mistake.
2. They openly try to help others.
3. They make other people feel important.

If you aren't already a giver, why not try that approach? Did you know that if you're not a "giver," some people may already be seeing you as a "taker"? It's true. And most of us dislike takers, don't we? Yet we hear them all the time...

1. "Can I *take* a moment of your time?"
2. "Take my word for it. It will only *take* a few minutes."
3. "Take it easy! I'm only going to take a loan application."
4. "I'm going to take a listing."

One day we're going to depart from this messy planet empty-handed, leaving all that we've taken behind. So why not leave this earth as a giver instead of as a taker? After all, by doing so, we not only help others but we also set an example for our children. Because the way we treat others today is how our children will one day treat others.

It's like the story of the poor farmer who struck it rich in the Mexican lottery. This farmer won $10 million, but he still made his father sleep in the barn! The farmer was somewhat ashamed of his father because of the old man's shabby clothes and the way that his father smelled.

One winter night, the farmer told his son Michael to fetch one of the horse blankets from the stable. The little boy did as he was told.

"What do you want me to do with this horse blanket?" asked Michael.

"I want you to give it to your grandfather," said the farmer.

"Why?"

"So he won't be cold tonight."

"Oh," said the little boy. Taking the blanket, little Michael grabbed a pair of scissors and started to cut the horse blanket in half, making two large pieces.

"What are you doing?" asked the farmer. "I said that's for your grandfather."

"Well, I'm saving half for you," said the little boy. "That

way, when you get to be his age and are living out in the barn, you won't be cold either."

The point is, how you treat others is how the children in your world will one day treat others. How you treat your parents when they get older is most likely how your children will treat you when you grow older. Children learn from our example.

IF THE WORST HAPPENS, LEARN FROM IT

If circumstances are such that you or someone you know endures a sale from hell, the best option is to recognize the problem, learn from it, lick your wounds, and move on. After all, successful people know that success isn't always built on success; it's also built on failure, frustration and sometimes total bankruptcy. As I've mentioned, the world that I know and love is a messy place. Hopefully you'll be more successful in your next real estate venture, and you will be able to smile as you gather around the dinner table and tell your children the "sale from hell" story.

Somebody wise once wrote, "Blessed are those who can laugh at themselves, for they shall never cease to be amused"!

Maybe that's the attitude to keep in mind if you are currently having a sale from hell real estate transaction—or if you have ever experienced an even worse nightmare in your life. As I've said before, the world is a messy place, often filled with problems—big, small, fat and tall ones! But it's not always the problem that's the problem. It's often how you deal with it. Your attitude is the key, and your understanding is the answer.

I'll jump off my soapbox now. Thank you for taking your time to read this book. In my family, when people leave, it's customary to give a hug or a kiss and exchange words about seeing one another again soon. It is with this same spirit that I bid you farewell and wish you the best of success in your next real estate transaction. Hopefully it won't be a sale from you-know-where!

BOOKS

For Sale by Owner in California, by George Devine, Nolo Press, copyright 1987-1999.

How to Sell Your Home in a Buyer's Market, Martin M. Shenkman & Warren Boroson, John Wiley & Sons Inc, copyright 1970.

What Clients Love:A Field Guide to Growing Your Business, by Harry Beckwith,Warner Books ©2003

Real Estate as a Second Language, by Roger Reitzel, illustrated by David J. Schutten, Chicago Review Press, copyright 1983. Contact Roger for speeches and seminars too, he's really a funny guy! (626) 675-7460.

MAGAZINES

Realtor magazine, www.realtor.org/realtormag

Money magazine, www.money.com This excellent website has lots of useful information including weather, ratings on cities, crime, economy, population and more.

INTERNET WEBSITES

www.realestatefocus.com: Realtor Jerry Fowler of South Carolina presents interesting and informative Southeastern horror stories. You don't have to live in South Carolina to appreciate the lessons imparted from these tales.

www.independentinspectors.org: A website that lists independent home inspectors of North America.

www.nolo.com: The Nolo Press website is filled with information for people to "do it yourself."

www.titleanswers.com: Presented by First American Title Company, this website offers interesting real-life examples of claims paid on behalf of the First American Title Company. There are some expensive lessons learned by people across the U.S.

www.BestPlaces.net: At this website, you'll find city information relating to: crime, climate, salary, schools, cost of living and more! An excellent resource for an investor or someone who is looking to relocate.

www.domania.com: Enter an address and you can find out how much the home is worth or how much it recently sold for.

GOVERNMENT WEB SITES

http://www.vahomes.org/: This website contains repossessed homes from the Department of Veteran's Affairs.

http://www.hud.gov/offices/hsg/sfh/reo/reobuyfaq.cfm This website contains FHA repos —repossessed homes from the Department of Housing & Urban Development. (HUD)

http://w3.pwgsc.gc.ca/govland/search-e.html: This website has Canadian public works and government repossessed homes.

http://www2.fdic.gov/drrore: This website features properties from the Federal Deposit Insurance Corporation. FDIC

http://www.propertydisposal.gsa.gov/property/: The property disposal website of the U.S. Government Services Administration.

http://www.treas.gov/auctions/customs/realprop.html: Seized residential real estate of the U.S. Department of Treasury can be found at this website.

http://www.usdoj.gov/marshals/assets/nsl.html: Find property forfeited under the U.S. Department of Justice.

http://www.resales.usda.gov/:This site includes foreclosed property and pending foreclosures of mostly rural property, houses and farms that can be purchased from the United States Department of Agriculture, USDA.

http://app1.sba.gov/pfsales/dsp_sum_rpt_by_state.cfm: The Small Business Administration offers commercial as well as residential foreclosures.

www.nsc.org/ehc/lead.htm: Offers lead-base paint information or call (800)424-LEAD.

• Index •

Acknowledgments

Special thanks to my friend and big brother JC and the people of Santa Clarita, CA who have endured me over the past 25 years. I appreciate your support!

To my Dad and Mom, "Thanks, I love you."

To Tom Hopkins who first taught me how to sell professionally, thank you.

To sales trainers Floyd Wickman, Mike Ferry, Barbara Schwartz, Mike Domer, Brian Buffini, Danielle Kennedy, Zig Ziglar, Joe Girard, and Og Mandino. Your material has inspired me to greater success.

Thank you Robin Q. and Rosie G. I couldn't have made this book without you!

To my beautiful wife Roxana, "I love you and appreciate everything you do for me."

To my sons, Brandon and Kevin, "I love you guys."

To my real estate guru, Jim Behan, "I'm always learning from you."

A word of appreciation to my family, Pat, Kevin,Jackie, Margo, Paula, Tom, Sean & Rosie Boog, and my adopted family—Richie & Mary Trimble, DC & Mary Clark, Mike & Tricia Scarnechia, Tony & Sheila Scarnechia, Timbo & Jen, Rob & Toni, Thomas, Marla, Kim, Kevin & Jackie Trimble.

Did you endure the "move from hell"?
C'mon, while you're still thinking about it, buy a T-shirt or coffee mug to celebrate surviving the ordeal!
Visit the Website:
www.movefromhell.com
to see all the cool products there.